PEOPLE ARE
unappealing

TRUE STORIES OF OUR

COLLECTIVE

CAPACITY

TO IRRITATE AND ANNOY

sara barron

PEOPLE ARE
unappealing*

*EVEN ME

THREE RIVERS PRESS

New York

Published in the United States by Three Rivers Press, an imprint of the
Crown Publishing Group, a division of Random House, Inc., New York.
www.crownpublishing.com

Three Rivers Press and the Tugboat design are registered trademarks of
Random House, Inc.

Library of Congress Cataloging-in-Publication Data

Barron, Sara.
   People are unappealing / Sara Barron.—1st ed.
      p. cm.
   1. Barron, Sara.   2. Comedians—United States—Biography.   I. Title.
   PN2287.B27A3 2009
   792.702'8092—dc22
   [B]   2008039915

ISBN 978-0-307-38245-0

Printed in the United States of America

DESIGN BY ELINA D. NUDELMAN

10 9 8 7 6 5 4 3 2

First Edition

FOR MY PARENTS,
LYNN AND JOE

CONTENTS

ACT III: **Hombres**

ACT IV: **Orthopedics**

ACT V: **Antichrist**

The experiences recounted in this book are real, but to protect the privacy and anonymity of those involved, I have changed names and identifying characteristics of everyone besides my family members and the inimitable Maggie McBrien. In some cases, I combined the characteristics and incidents of different people into one composite character. I have also rearranged, combined, and compressed events and time periods to streamline the story.

ACT I

suburbia

lady daddy

I've always preferred sedentary activities to active activities. In my tweenage years, I shirked anything labeled "extracurricular" for the chance to head home after school and sit locked in the bathroom. I preferred the bathroom to my bedroom because it had a lock on the door for much-needed privacy, and I'd spend my time there alternately cramming the ambiguous genitalia of my Barbie and Ken dolls together and interviewing myself about my imagined acting career. Pretending an electric toothbrush was a microphone, I'd ask, "What's it like being a movie star?"

"It's fun," I'd answer back. "Sometimes I have sex with John Stamos."

I'd sustain this clever banter until my father knocked on the door. My father is a creature of habit, so from Monday to Friday for eighteen years he arrived home from work at 5:32 P.M. First he'd set down his briefcase to file his nails, and then he'd "get lucky," to use the euphemism coined by my Metamucil addict of a mother. "What I wouldn't do for your father's small intestine," she says. "The man is blessed." He'd plan it this way since the use of public bathrooms always prompted his panicked descent into oblivion. "A person ought to be able to relax and enjoy himself," he'd say. "I like a little space, a little 'me' time. Is that so bizarre?"

So he'd oust me from the bathroom and I'd head downstairs to the living room, where he'd join me fifteen minutes later. "I feel like a new man!" he'd say, and then unwind with a bottle of blush wine and one of his many musical albums. By "musical albums" I do not mean, simply, albums. I'm not being redundant. I mean *musical* as in *musical*s: Marvin Hamlisch. Kander. Ebb. "Are you listening to this?!" he'd ask over the blare of the title song from *Oklahoma!* "Doesn't it just . . . gosh! I don't know . . . doesn't it make you want to dance?!" Then with the flourish of an imaginary cape, he'd twirl his hips in tight, concentric circles.

Usually it's a father who catches the seed of a lisp in his son or a talent for eyeballing another man's inseam, and he bristles with fear at the prospect of, to quote my next-door neighbor Brian, whose childhood pillowcases were sewn from tattered Confederate flags, "some gay shit." That my father could recite the entire oeuvre of Rodgers and Hammerstein, that his sock drawer was flecked with freesia potpourri, forced my younger brother, Sam, into the reverse situation.

"Sometimes Daddy's like a lady," Sam would say.

This was true. But it didn't faze me. On the contrary, my dad's offbeat behavior left me feeling optimistic. "At least if Dad's gay," I pointed out, "he's not doing Mom."

My mother, in a pair of heels with her hair teased, has a good eight inches on my dad. Size-wise, they look like Golden Girls Bea Arthur and Estelle Getty, respectively, a resemblance emphasized by my mother's affection for tunics and my father's clothing staple, a shapeless, taupe cardigan. Parents and sex is an unhappy combination for most, and with their atypical height discrepancy *and* the fashion taste of Floridian retirees, I've always found the notion especially upsetting. If they weren't having sex—and if my father's weak wrists and sibilant *s* were to blame—it was no skin

14

off my back. My parents were among the few still married in our Jewish suburb of Chicago, and while in later years I'd come to appreciate this fact, when I was young, the notion of divorced parents struck me as chic. Very *now*. The possibility of two separate homes seemed wonderfully decadent, and I wished for divorce in the hope that one of them might land someone with a heated pool.

"You should've seen the way Dad was eyeing Dr. Cohen," I'd tell my mom after a father-daughter visit to the dentist. "He kept saying how much he liked his tie. Then his shoes. It was . . . I don't know . . . *weird*."

"Nice try," she'd say. "Your dad's not doing Dr. Cohen."

Elsewhere, a father of questionable sexual orientation cripples a family into silence. But not us. Father: gay-seeming. Mother: psychotherapist. This is the woman who coined the phrase "Don't repress, instead express!" So we discussed it over dinner, the conversation underscored by the '70s Broadway blockbuster *A Chorus Line*.

"Listen to the lyrics," instructed my father. "It's a song about chasing your dreams. I hope you both chase *your* dreams." Then his eyes would glass over.

"Dad's a homo!" Sam would shout. "He cries like a homo!"

"Your father's not gay," my mother chimed in. "He's effeminate."

"Oh, *I'm* gay!" my father countered. "Who here knows what *gay* really means?"

He writes dictionary definitions for a living, my father. Never in your life have you met someone more enthused about alternate meanings.

"Homo!" Sam shouted.

"And?"

"Happy," my mother offered. "Your father's happy and effeminate."

Effeminate? Yes. Happy? Debatable. His affinity for losing himself in the canon of American show tunes and drowning what remained of the day in bottles of blush wine didn't scream

15

"happy!" or "fulfilled!" Here was a man who'd endured great sacrifice. His childhood ambition had been to be the next Edith Piaf. The morphine addiction and untimely death weren't of interest. "But my goodness!" he'd say in later years as he hummed a tune about a swarthy French cadet. "What a voice! What charisma!" He spent years studying her lyrics and emotive performance style but was forced to abandon the dream once he married my mother.

"Oh no," she told him. "Not on my time, you don't. You pack up the records and brandy snifter and you go find yourself a real job."

Like a hospice worker unperturbed if her kid gets the flu, my mother the therapist was none too moved by the average emotional trauma. You spend your days regaled with stories of molestation, battery, and molestation *and* battery, and your skin grows thick. You don't worry yourself if you crush a grown man's dream of being Edith Piaf. "Up by the bootstraps," you tell him, and—as marriage must be built on compromise—you shut your mouth when he encourages your children to reenact *Miss Saigon* in the backyard.

When someone asked if she found my father's atypically ladylike ways at all disturbing, my mother, unconcerned, would say, "Joe is a wonderful husband and father," and then, to put such people in their place for having had the nerve to pry, she'd add, "*and* he's more regular than a billboard on a highway! He's to be envied and admired!"

My parents' utter lack of defensiveness is the best reason I can give as to why I *do* believe my father's straight. I stand behind that age-old slogan "the one who smelt it dealt it." I believe the repressed homosexuals of the world are too busy Bible thumping and slinging words like *fag* around to be entranced by *South Pacific*.

Upon my eleventh birthday and junior high school entrée, my father predictably insisted that I audition for the school musical.

"Just think of it!" he cooed. "The smell of the greasepaint! The roar of the crowd!"

Up until that point I had, as previously mentioned, harbored an aversion to extracurricular activities, preferring instead to hang out in my bathroom with my Barbie dolls or on the living room couch eating loaves of bread. Despite these natural inclinations, my father had intermittently tried to engage me in different "fun" projects. Would I like to learn to ride a bike? To swim? Perhaps it would amuse me to play Maria to his Mother Abbess? But I declined each offer, preferring instead to read a Harlequin romance or, in later years, masturbate. But the school musical suggestion *did* pique my interest. It was the bit about the "roaring" crowd that did it. My father's passion had instilled in me not only a knowledge of musical theater, but also a desire to be on stage or screen myself. It was true I lacked a decent singing voice, but I compensated for this disadvantage with an uncanny ability to mimic Tina Turner's dancing. Call it what you will—luck? the grace of god?—I knew it earned me the right to an audience. I always assumed my singing could improve with practice, and in the meantime, I'd wow a crowd with a hair toss to "Proud Mary." During my aforementioned on-toilet interviews of myself *by* myself, I'd pose questions regarding this wide array of talents.

"Ms. Barron," I'd say into the electric toothbrush, "what's it like to be so young and so accomplished?"

Then I'd smile politely, feigning discomfort at this limelight thrust upon me. "I've been so very blessed," I'd say. "God gave me this talent. Now it's my job to share it with the world."

A stage seemed preferable to a porcelain bowl if we're talking decent platforms for attracting attention to oneself, so I decided to give it a shot. I told my father I'd audition, "But only if you'll buy me a microphone."

"Absolutely not," shouted my mother, who'd overheard the conversation from the kitchen. "We do *not* reward with material goods in this family."

My father shrugged. The only thing he loved more than musical theater was avoiding conflict with my mother.

"You heard the woman!" he shouted back for her benefit. But then to me he whispered, "How's about I promise you the microphone for Hanukkah instead?"

"Deal," I said.

"Deal," he said. "Just promise not to tell your mother."

The show was *Guys and Dolls*, and I auditioned in a Bart Simpson T-shirt tucked into gym shorts, performing an a cappella rendition of the up-tempo but soulful "Chain of Fools." I landed the role of Sakiko. *Sakiko?* you're thinking. In *Guys and Dolls*? Yes. If you blink, you miss her, but she's there in the show's opening Times Square montage. In the movie version, she appears as a tourist more Hawaiian than Asian, draped in leis and a floral-pattern dress, in a shtick most aptly described as "The City Is Big and Confusing! I Like to Laugh!"

As someone pinkish and pale and covered in moles, someone once told by a Bulgarian dry cleaner that I had hair "like that of belonging to the nest of birds. Yes! Nests of the stork!" I can say with great certainty: I do not look Asian. I do not look maybe Asian. My associations to the continent are limited to the facts that in avoidance of processed carbs, I eat a lot of sashimi, and that in the early '00s I got a case of HPV from a Vietnamese sculptor I'd been dating named Quong. But that's it. And as a result, Sakiko and I seemed an unlikely pair. She wasn't at all what I'd had in mind when I auditioned. At the very least, I'd hoped for a dance solo: a box step or grapevine performed with a line of chorus girls behind me. But Sakiko? Shuffling along and laughing like an asshole at a painted-on-burlap version of the Chrysler Building? No, thank you.

When my father arrived home from work later that night, he could smell my disappointment. He's astute that way, sensitive to others. I broke the news of Sakiko, Asian Tourist #2, and he tried desperately to comfort me. "Oh now, honey," he'd said. "Don't be disappointed! You know, there's an old saying in the theater that goes, 'There are no small parts. Just small actors.'"

"Who thought that up?" asked my mom.

"I don't know *who* exactly," he answered. "It's just a thing that people say."

"Well, it sounds like crap to me. Crap drummed up by someone repressing his anger. Sara"—she turned to me—"if you'd rather spend your afternoons on the toilet talking to yourself about . . ."

"My future in showbiz."

"Fine. Your 'future in showbiz.' If you'd rather do that than this Sakiko thing, you be my guest." She fluffed her hair, threw on a poncho, and looked at her watch. "Oy!" she cried. "I'm late. I have a six o'clock appointment with a client who's terrified of—get this—goats!"

I appreciated her support even though I knew it stemmed less from an interest in encouraging my natural talents and more from her need to save money. My mother is shockingly frugal—her idea of "treating herself" involves the purchase of brand-name stool softener—and the moment I handed over a costume list that read "leotard, chopsticks, kimono," she got angry.

"This is absurd!" she shouted. "Do these teachers think parents have kimonos and leotards just lying around? I'm not shelling out my hard-earned money so my daughter can look Asian for a two-night run of *Guys and Dolls*!"

Spending money goes against her natural instincts. But rather than sling a word like *cheap* or *Jew* around, I try to focus on the nobility inherent in her habit. Our suburb teemed with wealth—Range Rovers, uptalk, I knew a dog with a masseuse—and all she wanted was to keep her children grounded. Sam and I were kept on close watch lest we develop a taste for life's finer aspects.

"First you want a microphone for god-knows-what, then it's a pony, then the next thing you know, you'll need a goddamn maid to wipe your ass!"

I didn't think a microphone was the first step on the road to incompetence. But my mother begged to differ. On this purchase, on every other. Normally I viewed her refusals as the chance to sulk or slam a door, but this time it was cause for celebration. No kimono? No Sakiko.

"Oh well," I told my dad once my mother left for work. "So I guess I'll just drop out? I think it's no big deal? Since the rehearsals haven't started yet?" I swung up the end of every sentence and nodded my head yes in a subtle suggestion, a secular prayer: Please. Don't make me go. Let me stay at home instead dueting with my brother bits of *Cats* for your amusement. Let me lie prostrate on the couch, a loaf of French bread in my mouth.

"Now that sounds like a quitter talking!" my father answered back. "Not a showbiz starlet headed to the top." He paced around the room before turning to face my brother and me. "Who here knows what the word *resourceful* means?"

I sighed and Sam passed gas.

"Excuse you," said my father. "*Resourceful* means *inventive*. Or *clever*. It means that we can pull a costume together even if we can't spend money. *We* can be . . . resourceful!"

Too lazy to battle my father's enthusiasm, I followed him upstairs to my mother's closet, where he found a floor-length silk robe—"Voilà: kimono!" he squealed—and also a sea horse–spattered bathing suit from 1985. "Well, well, well," he said. "It looks like we've found ourselves a leotard."

We ordered Chinese food that night so I'd have a pair of chopsticks. Having finished the meal, my father lathered his set in the sink, then laid them down to dry in the dish rack.

"Look out, Sakiko," he said in a voice like a soap-opera star. He was confident. Cunning. Here was a man with a trick up his sleeve. "Here comes Sara Barron."

The next day I attended my first after-school rehearsal. Directing the production was Ms. Manishevitz, the school's drama teacher. I didn't know how old she was—young enough for pigtails; old enough for pigtails to emphasize a bald spot—and I didn't care. I couldn't invest the time in trying to figure it out because I was too frequently distracted by her nostrils. A half-inch long and a millimeter wide, they looked like mail slots and were, by far, the most compelling set I'd ever seen. You could forget what day it was looking at these things, and until you got used to them, until they ceased to surprise you, it was easy to ignore the other offsetting facets of their owner. You could ignore the fact that judging by the rest of her appearance, Ms. Manishevitz thought she was heading out not for a day teaching drama to children ages eleven to fourteen, but rather to Burning Man or back a few decades to Woodstock. Someplace for hippies to gather and swap rain sticks and chlamydia. Her accessories featured an impressive amount of hemp and highlighted the obvious absence of a brassiere. A tie-dyed bandanna she felt naked without, an array of floor-length peasant skirts that turned transparent in fluorescent light. Underarms like lint collectors. How she got away with these sorts of fashion antics surrounded on all sides by tweens chomping at the bit for someone to humiliate? Faculty who knew enough to wear brassieres? I can only think it's because we were all too taken with her nose to notice.

The first day of rehearsal, Ms. Manishevitz sat Indian-style in the junior high school gymnasium, her breasts grazing a set of conga drums she'd crammed between her legs. "Welcome!" she bellowed as each student arrived. Then she started banging on the congas. "Now move to the music!" she shouted. "Everybody!"

Jewish preadolescents are not the most adept when it comes to improvising movement to African rhythms. We all just eyed each other uncomfortably and then started shifting our weight from one foot to the other. This wasn't what Ms. Manishevitz had in mind. "No, no, *no*!" she screamed. "Like *this*!" She set the congas down and walked toward the center of the room, where she started grunting. Low, guttural moans you'd attribute to the coming or going of an object in a body. "Uh uh uhhhhh," she panted. "Ah ya ya ya ya." Then she did a series of squats and, seemingly pleased with herself, returned to her spot on the floor. "*That,*" she said, "is how it's done."

We followed up the demonstration with a game of tag and spent the remainder of the hour listening to Ms. Manishevitz tell stories about her former acting conquests, including the time she'd starred in a Bay Area community theater production of *Guys and Dolls* herself. "People knew I had talent," she said, "but talent alone didn't get me all the way."

What was "all the way"? An unpaid '80s acting role? The job of teaching theater to children transfixed by her nostrils?

A forty-minute recitation of her résumé ensued. Highlights included bossy orphan Pepper in *Annie*, Rum Tum Tugger in *Cats*. Teaching drum lessons to the elderly, mime class for convicts. "What can I say?" she went on. "I've been blessed as both Teacher and Performer. We all have different gifts, and these are mine. And it's my pleasure to be here to share those gifts with you."

Certain people have a knack for speaking about themselves in the least engaging way possible. Prompted by a simple question— "How are you?" "Is that your dog?"—they can preach a story of self-aggrandizing minutiae so boring, a steak knife to the eye is made to seem suddenly, surprisingly pleasant. These types, lacking in no particular order (1) self-awareness, (2) charm, (3) sensitivity, can't be steered off track, and over time I've learned the most effective course of action in dealing with them is to allow one's mind to wander. Ms. Manishevitz rambled on until I began to imagine a microscopic version of myself scaling her chin, then sliding deftly into her nostrils like a quarter in a slot machine. Once inside, I'd discover a fairy-tale terrain peopled with snow queens and satyrs.

"Hello, Sara!" they'd say. "Welcome to our land. Might you like a peppermint surprise?"

In my mind's eye, I'd been napping in the shade of an edible butterscotch tree when all of a sudden Ms. Manishevitz snapped me back to reality. She was handing out rehearsal schedules while instructing us to share what we'd learned that day.

"I've shared a lot of myself," she said. "Now it's your turn." Then she clasped her hands at her sternum and bowed her head. She looked poised for a flurry of spontaneous applause but would, it seemed, have to settle instead on the solicited compliments of middle schoolers. Given the chance, some chomped at the bit to bury a nose in her ass. "How excited I am for the show!" said one. "That the show will take a lot of work, but it'll be worth it!" said another. But I, for one, went neutral. I said, "You like drums." If my answer underwhelmed her, so what? What could she do? Take away the dance solo I'd been denied in the first place? Please.

At least playing Sakiko meant I didn't have a lot to lose. And at least I'd have a light rehearsal schedule. Sakiko appeared only in the opening and closing musical numbers, so I figured I'd have a few of these bang-on-a-drum sessions, a few to learn the title song, then maybe a dress rehearsal toward the end. Of course, my father insisted on at-home rehearsals in addition, but these were a piece of cake seeing as how I'd just lock myself in my room, then do as I pleased—interview myself about myself, mount my stuffed hippo Stuart—and no one knew the difference. Asked to share what I'd been working on at dinner, I'd simply belt out a song from *Guys and Dolls* in the style of Edith Piaf. This was enough to keep my father happy. My mother, on the other hand, developed this habit of wearing what she called her "dinner earplugs."

"It's not that you're not good," she'd say as she nuzzled them into her ears. "You are. It's just, sometimes you sing so loud, it makes me *feel* angry." She preferred to tune out while I sang Piaf-style and my father conducted my brother's musical accompaniment on the recorder.

On the eve of opening night, I sat locked in my bedroom. Having promised my father a diligent rehearsal, I'd spent a half hour gnawing at my forearm (I imagined it to be John Stamos), when all of a sudden I got my period for the first time. It might be a universal experience for half of us, but that doesn't mean it's not jarring. *My goodness,* you think, that's *different*. I'm of the opinion that the details of the experience belong in a different book with a different cover—mine would sport a Georgia O'Keeffe reproduction and the title *A Journey into Womanhood*—but I've included the anecdote only so I might explain how it was that my forthcoming stage debut included a sanitary pad. And a bathing suit.

My crotch looked like a Ken doll's.

"Oh, look at you!" gasped my father when he saw me descending the stairs. "You look like a real Broadway star!"

Sam, who stood beside my father, added, "You have a penis like my penis!"

"Your sister does *not* have a penis!" my mother shouted in

23

response. A less direct woman would have left it at that, but she believes in being honest, in telling the whole story. "She only *looks* like she does because she's in a puffy sanitary pad."

As we've gotten older, I've learned to trust my brother. Unmoved by other people's opinions, he possesses the self-confidence to facilitate total and objective honesty. My mother tries, but her occasional jabs at sensitivity affect the skill. If I really want to know—"Is my hair thinning?" "Can you smell that?"—I ask Sam. If he says yes, it means yes. If he says, "You look like you have a penis," it means I look like I have a penis. And a pubescent female who looks like she has a penis ought not to appear in front of an audience.

But no one in my family had the wherewithal to make that call.

In my debut performance later that night, I'd just begun my opening procession across the stage when the silk tie came undone on my mother's old robe, forcing it open. My strangely ambiguous, Lycra-clad genitals were exposed for all to see.

The crowd went wild.

"That chick's got a dick!" someone shouted.

"Chick with a dick *alert*!" another joined in.

One of the problems with a phrase like "chick with a dick" is that it lends itself to chanting. "That young woman looks like she has a penis!" wouldn't work so well, but "chick with a dick" has a nice ring to it, and as such, the first few rows joined together in one happy, rousing chorus: "Chick with a dick! Chick with a dick!"

My father hadn't waited twelve years for my stage debut only to sit in the back of a theater and listen to my peers shout about my penis. He waited twelve years for my stage debut and sat in the *front* of a theater, sandwiched between my mother and brother. I imagine he managed the trauma with a convenient lie. *Everything happens for a reason,* he must have told himself. Or perhaps he pictured a young Edith Piaf singing on the streets of Paris being pelted with rotten tomatoes. Perhaps he decided my rocky beginning would only serve to make me stronger, only grant me greater appreciation for my forthcoming achievements.

Taking action against my assailants was left to my brother. In a falsetto that carried over all the other voices, he yelled, "NO, SHE DOESN'T! SARA HAS A VAGINA!"

One of the problems with a phrase like "Sara has a vagina," when it follows a chant to the contrary, is that everyone who isn't belly laughing at your expense already now has just cause to join in.

I had no idea what to do, what with everyone carrying on about my penis, then my vagina. So I smiled. Sakiko smiled. And walked herself offstage.

On the car ride home we played a game called "At Least It's Not." Invented by my mother, it's supposed to help you keep perspective when the going gets rough; when, for example, you're publicly labeled a pre-op tranny because you have a large pubic bone and a heavy period.

"At least it's not cancer," said my mother. "And at least you do have a vagina, just like Sam said. At least you're not a hermaphrodite. Now *that'd* be no walk in the park, am I right?"

"At least she has a vagina!" Sam repeated.

"We did that one already."

"At least it's not a comment on your talent," my father pointed out. "I mean, wouldn't it have been worse if you'd been booed for your singing?"

"That's true!" affirmed my mom. "And at least the pad didn't fall out onstage. Imagine the mess! Now you do one."

I searched hard for perspective, some way in which things could be worse. I said, "At least I won't ever have to do that show again."

My father's first instinct when I said this was to sling another adage of enthusiasm at me. "You can't give up that easy!" he said.

But couldn't I? I mean, I *had* just been emotionally sabotaged, and having lived vicariously through me, he must have felt equally saddened and exhausted. I think he lacked the drive to force me

25

through another show. "Oh, all right," he sighed a moment later. "There'll always be next year I suppose, and maybe then you won't be struggling with"—and here he broke off in search of the appropriate word choice—"quite the . . . same . . . problems."

"It's called 'her period,'" my mother corrected. "It's not a problem. It's an egg."

"FROM HER VAGINA!" Sam yelled.

"Not quite," she answered, "but close."

The next night I propositioned Ms. Manishevitz. Backstage before the show, I asked if I might skip the opening number. "I could empty the garbage instead," I said, "or tidy up the restrooms."

Distracted as she was by my now infamous "dick," she struggled to maintain eye contact. Her gaze kept darting down. "Um, sure," she said. "Garbage or bathrooms. Whichever you'd prefer."

Playing Sakiko in your middle-school production of *Guys and Dolls* doesn't count for much if posted on your résumé, but at least no one will miss you when you're gone. And at least the show will close the day after it opens. Called "chick with a dick" one night, Windexing faucets in the ladies' room the next. But then at least it's over. Then at least you can return to your old routine of evenings spent on the toilet, talking to yourself about yourself, envisioning a level of success you'd always lack the talent to achieve.

"Ms. Barron," I began, "share with us, if you don't mind"— and I'd shake my head. Of course not. That's why I was there: to share, to teach—"some of the struggles young actors must expect to face."

For a moment, I'd feign a search for those old memories. "It *is* hard in the beginning," I'd say. "You'll play to hostile crowds, endure humiliations: the jokes about the penis you don't have, the occasions when your brother shouts 'VAGINA!' to defend you . . ."

"And then?"

"Well, then you move on. Then—if you learn, as *I* have learned, to be resourceful—you'll find new and different ways to shame yourself." I flushed the toilet. "It's par for the course if you want to be an entertainer."

2

you say "penis."
i say "pienus."

Every year my mother hosts Thanksgiving dinner. The only person she invites besides my father, my brother, and me is my grandmother, her widowed mother, Natalie. I've never been partial to grandparental nicknames. "Nana." "Bubbie." I have a friend who calls his grandma "Bop Bop." These terms of endearment always strike me as too cutesy for the elderly. So I call Natalie simply "Grandma."

She calls me "a disappointment."

"What a disappointment," she'll say, "that you . . ."

Fill in the blank.

". . . have that acne on your chest," or ". . . like to date the Negroes."

My brother's done a better job of eschewing her criticisms over the years—I imagine she can't sniff out his vulnerability in the same way she does mine—and my dad she just ignores. Sometimes if he fares poorly at a prototypically masculine task like jar-opening or turkey-carving, she'll call him "Mr. Incompetent," but that's the extent of it. It's my mother and I who serve as verbal punching bags. I've always craved an explanation as to why.

"*Why?!*" I'd cry once my grandmother left. "*Why* is she like that? *Why* must I always be attacked?"

"It's how she shows she loves you," my mother would say. "She's just . . . what's that word you kids say? Oh! Fronting! That's it! She's just fronting!" That rationale may work for my mother, but it doesn't work for me. Someone says, "You look pregnant in those jeans," and I don't feel loved. I feel like swapping someone's denture cream with cyanide or opting for elastic waistbands in the future, but a warm wash of affection is rarely the prevailing theme.

I was sixteen years old when I finally figured out the loophole in my grandmother's behavior: She'd soften significantly if she'd had a drink. A couple Jack and gingers, and a comment like "Have you gained weight?" would morph into "You *may* have gained weight . . . but you still look cute to Grandma!" She'd be warm, affectionate, supportive. She'd let down her guard, abandon the resentments built up from having a husband who died young and the decades of ensuing widowhood. You'd just have to liquor her up. So I'd liquor her up. At family holidays, my mother would cook, my father would clean, Sam would watch the static covering the soft-core porn on the cable channels we didn't get, and I'd watch my grandma's rocks glass like a hawk. I'd sit poised with a bottle of Jack, making sure it stayed filled to the brim. I'd say, "Grandma, you look thirsty!" and she'd respond, "Oh, twist my arm!" It was an effective call-and-response that kept her in adequate spirits.

Until recently.

See, now she's eighty-six and on a handful of meds that all forbid drinking. So she must be endured, now and forever, au naturel at family functions. It's been a rough readjustment. My mother has handled it better than I have. When, for example, my grandma says, "Your brisket smells like garbage," my mom just laughs it off. "That's just Sam," she'll joke. "He hasn't showered in days! He's been too busy watching static-covered porn!" Well, *I* think it's funny and so does Sam, but all we get from Grandma is a gagging noise and a follow-up snort of disgust.

I've learned to run for cover. Following her annual Thanksgiving arrival, I stick around just long enough to hug hello, then feign a flare-up of my irritable bowel syndrome and hightail it to my bedroom, where I hide for the night. (I developed IBS in the mid '90s and have leaned on it ever since as an excuse for, well, everything. Forget a school assignment? Late for work? Angry grandma? I blame IBS. People never ask for follow-up details once you say the word *bowel*. It's perfect.) On one such evening several years ago, I did exactly this, sticking myself in my bedroom at 5:00 P.M. after she told me, "Your love handles are strange!" Here, I napped for awhile and then—faced with the terrifying absence of a television—I decided to read for a change. I searched the bookshelves until my thumb passed the binding of a tattered spiral notebook. I pulled it from the shelf and realized it was a diary I'd kept some ten years prior. I opened to a random page and read.

Then I take his pienus and rub my face in it.

This surprised me. While I'd correctly identified it as a diary, I'd anticipated something more like, "Today was fun. I went swimming."

"Then I take his pienus and rub my face in it" had thrown me off guard. It's when I realized: This was *The Porn*.

The Porn is a screenplay I wrote when I was twelve years old, springing hair from new places and packing sanitary pads into swimsuits. Fifty pages long, it's riddled with eight pornographic sex scenes, each one described in greater and more graphic detail than the last, each one imagined from the perspective of an inexperienced, sexually frustrated preadolescent. I start with

"Hey! Wanna French?" but advance quickly to "He humped me wildly with his wiener." I swear I thought I'd burned it, but apparently not. Apparently, my parents preserved it in my childhood bedroom, where it sits studded with the beady eyes of a dozen unicorn stickers.

As a tween, my preferred literary genre was romance. I whipped through Judith Krantz's oeuvre by age twelve, and—perhaps as an homage? I can't be sure. I can't *quite* remember my specific motivations save for a set of raging hormones—I eventually decided to write one for myself, a little something to call my own in avoidance of library due dates. *The Porn* is what resulted. Of course, *The Porn* was not the original title. That came later, born from the comment of a friend who'd read it and declared, "IT'S PORN! YOU WROTE PORN!" Its original title was *Rosewood Beach*. Rosewood Beach is a local beach in my hometown where, at age ten, I was flashed by a man in a trench coat and Cubs hat. For years, I thought: Rosewood Beach = Penis. Like peanut butter, jelly. Ketchup, mustard. Rosewood Beach, penis. Hence the title. The protagonist was a young woman I named Jenny Wilkinson, and her myriad of love interests were Mark Brolin, Jim Henley, and Brian. Brian had no last name. The only follow-up detail I give is that he'd only have sex if Michael Bolton's '91 smash album *Time, Love and Tenderness* was playing.

"Why don't you take off that real sexy leather skirt," he says in scene 5. "We can get in my convertible. I got this Michael Bolton tape."

"Okay," answers Jenny. "I feel like some real wild humping anyway."

The first page of *The Porn* includes a cast list. I cast Christie Brinkley in the role of Jenny Wilkinson and Tom Cruise in the role of Mark Brolin. Christie Brinkley? Fine. But Tom Cruise? Upsetting. All that enters my head when I think Tom Cruise these days is Scientology and a wide variety of things relating to the anus, e.g., hamsters, and so it disturbs me to see evidence of a time period in which I found him sexy. (I blame the *Risky Business* dance sequence and the iconic vision of Tommy's Hanes-covered crotch.) My character descriptions explain that Jenny is the most popular girl in high school and that Mark is the captain of the football team. Obviously, this means they ought to have a lot of intercourse. And they do. Here is Jenny's description of their first night together:

> *I swichted myself around so my head was right on his pienus, and I made my legs go into a squating position and made so he exactly saw up my viginia. So I am lying on top of him and he is humping me so hard I'm nearly flying off him. Then I take his pienus and rub my face and in it. Then I grab it in my two hand rub it all over.*

I believe I may have meant to write, "Then I take his penis and rub my face *in* it. Then I grab it in my two hand*s and* rub it all over my body." I also believe that I may have meant *penis* and *vagina* in lieu of the more exotically spelled *pienus* and *viginia*. But who knows? If nothing else, I stayed consistent, spelling penis *pienus* thirty-six times throughout. I know because I've counted.

Spelling aside, *The Porn* has other errors. Rereading it from an adult's perspective I realized that as a twelve-year-old I was confused about the following:

1. I thought that all penises were shaped like hooks. I know this because I make frequent reference to the verb *unhook*. As in, "Then I unhooked myself from his wiener." Now in later years, I would have sex with a gent whose pienus bent right in so bizarre and dramatic a fashion, it would be fair to describe it as hook-*like*. But experience has taught me said gent was an exception, not a rule.

2. I was convinced that all couples enjoyed a postcoital champagne toast. As far as I knew, where there's sex, there would be bubbly. "That was very nice," Jenny tells Mark in scene 8.

"Now I'm going to go get the champagne." It's not the mix of sex and alcohol that I find odd, it's the champagne-specific focus. Several awkward stints as a bridesmaid notwithstanding, champagne has been notably absent from my amour-making, personally. Beer, the occasional Zima in my younger days, these are my more frequent costars.

3. I was convinced an erection meant you *couldn't* have sex. "Jim's erection is out of control!" declares the narrator in scene 13. "Jenny tries to use her hand to calm it down before the problem gets any worse!" The last time I checked, erections weren't a problem. I mean, they *are* a problem if spotted out in public or on a relative. But in the privacy of a bedroom, I, for one, encourage them. Enough experience with enough alcoholics (see above) and you cultivate a fine appreciation of the item/event.

4. I was confused by orgasms. Arousal, I understood. I understood that there was this whole new set of feelings, that there was a momentum to said feelings, that they would build and build until . . . what? Something, I knew. I *knew* there'd be some sort of release. But, conceptually speaking, orgasms are awfully strange before you have them, and I couldn't hammer out logistically what exactly the release could be. So instead, *my* characters pee. Everywhere. They urinate all over the place as their alternate means of release. "I was at my peak of heat," Jenny tells her friend Carrie (the actress for the part included in the cast list? Paula Abdul), "and so I peed on him. Everywhere."

"And then?" prods Carrie.

"Well, then I cleaned it up with the help of my boobs. And then I went and got us some champagne."

When the ladies excuse themselves from this particular conversation, it's so Carrie can go have sex with her boyfriend, Zach. (My cast list names Kirk Cameron as the ideal actor for the role. And while nowadays it doesn't arouse me per se to picture Kirk

Cameron and Paula Abdul "hotly rubbing their genitals together in a circular motion" in quite the way it did in 1991, it does make a rerun of *Growing Pains* or *American Idol* much more fun to watch.) Meanwhile, Jenny heads to the local concert arena to have sex with a rock star named Jim Henley. This is the by-product, I assume, of my early-'90s obsession with *Don* Henley. Jim is passing through Jenny's hometown for a one-night-only appearance, and in *The Porn*'s final scene he tells his "butler" Hank, "Yo, Hank! Get me that sexy girl. Ya know, that one in the biker shorts and lacy bra." He means Jenny of course, and she obliges. The two then spend an hour "humping wildly on a steaming, bearskin rug," and in the end, Jim pees.

Jenny, however, does not. This makes Jenny angry.

"Well, now I gotta go," she fumes.

"That's too bad," says Jim, "since, ya know, it's been so satisfying."

"Maybe for you," says Jenny, "but not for me. Bye-bye."

Those are the two final lines of *The Porn,* and I find them shockingly realistic. Especially seeing as how the rest of it, what with its champagne toasts and noted appreciation of flaccidity, flies directly in the face of sexual realism. Real-life sex never unfolds as seamlessly; real-life partners aren't ever as dashing as a young Tom Cruise or Kirk Cameron. And I'd never pee in lieu of an orgasm. Well, I shouldn't say "never." I should say *"don't usually"*: I *don't usually* pee in lieu of an orgasm. And when I do, it's only ever because I've had too much beer to drink. *Beer,* I said. Or maybe Zima. But never champagne.

ONCE YOU'VE REVIEWED a graphic manifestation of your prepubescent desires, you don't usually feel like spending time around your family. But on this particular occasion, I'd been isolated for hours, stuck in a mind-bending warp of hook-shaped, counterproductive erections, and so my impulse, as strange as it sounds, *was* to share it with my family. I knew that if I read the perfect excerpt, they'd be wowed by my innate creative impulse. *I mean,* anyone *can steal a peak at a* Playboy, they'd think, *but it takes real moxie to pen fifty-one pages all on your own! Our gal is something special!* Suffice it to say that in choosing the excerpt, I'd avoid any mention of "rubbing a pienus all over my body," opting instead for something more PG, a description of Jenny's biker shorts in scene 8, let's say, or Brian's Speedo underwear from scene 4, in which he plays his Michael Bolton tape again.

Porn in hand, I dashed downstairs to find my grandmother packing leftovers into a Macy's shopping bag. "Well, look who it is," she growled, "Miss 'Irritation Bowels.'"

"Irri*table,*" I corrected.

Sam was the first to notice the spiral notebook. "What's that?" he asked, and pulled it from my hands before I could stop him. He opened to a random page. "'Jim grabbed her boobs and squeezed her butt,'" he read, "'while they humped real hard.'"

Herein lay the problem. I hadn't planned on Sam choosing the initial excerpt to be read aloud, on the immediate reveal of a butt squeeze or hard hump. "Give that *back,*" I ordered. But he refused. Reading those first few phrases, Sam smelled correctly the chance to humiliate me. And now, no matter the cost—an awkward cross of sex and family—he was prepared to pursue it.

"'Oh baby, oh Jenny,'" he laughed, "'hump me. Hump me. Satisfy me with your . . .'" And here he furrowed his brow. "*Vagina?*" he asked, now breathless from hysterics. "Is that supposed to say *vagina?*"

"Yes," I huffed. "*Vagina.* Now give it *back.*"

Just recently, I polled myself *about* myself and determined that I have three special talents. The first two are impressions (Tina Turner and also Kim Cattrall as Samantha on *Sex and the City*) and the third is my knack for misjudgment. No matter how shocked/amused/impressed I was with *The Porn,* it should've been glaringly obvious that sharing it *with my family* would result only in discomfort. Theirs? Mine? Both? Who knows. The possibilities were endless. My problem is, I always arrive at these moments of understanding five minutes too late. I don't realize that the revelation of my pubescent pornographic ramblings paves the path to embarrassment rather than to glory until *after* my brother gets hysterical at a phrase like "I switched myself around so my face was on his wiener." That's when I know I've misjudged.

My father couldn't hear our conversation, stuck as he was in the kitchen washing dishes to the *Pippin* soundtrack, but my mother and brother couldn't contain themselves.

"How *funny*!" said my mom. "What's next?"

"'THEN I WAS IN SO MUCH HEAT,'" Sam roared, "'I PEED ON HIM!'"

"GIVE IT *BACK*!" I screamed again. I lunged at him to try to wrestle it away, but he dashed back behind my father's stereo. "GIVE IT BACK!" I repeated. "SOMEONE MAKE HIM GIVE IT BACK!"

Now, usually my grandmother and I can't find a piece of common ground, but here she got behind me. "Stop this nonsense," she told him. "I don't want to hear about people urinating when I'm looking at a bowl of soup."

"Grandma's right!" I yelled. The words felt all at once uncomfortable but also instinctive. Like vomiting. "Listen to Grandma!"

I never thought my first sense of intergenerational connection would stem from a phrase like "I was in so much heat, I peed on him," but for me and *my* grandma, it's what worked. It's what finally brought us closer.

"Sam, you give that back," she instructed. "Sara's got enough to worry about, what with the irritated bowels."

"Thank you, Grandma."

"And whatever it is that's happening to her hair."

"What?" I asked. "What's happening to my hair?"

"It's started thinning at the crown. From behind you look like grandpa did in 1982."

So the bond was tenuous, but at least it was there: a possibility.

No one acknowledged my creative genius that night. Sam got a laugh and a Xeroxed copy of *The Porn* as a Hanukkah present the following year. My mother started using the word *pienus* exclusively in lieu of *penis*. "Did you hear about the man who had five pienuses?" begins her favorite joke. "His pants fit him like a glove!" And I got a whisker-thin strand of a connection to my grandma, the memory of the possibility that the perfect storm of pienuses and my misjudgment could unite us. Now I know the formula, and I await the next occasion.

3

first we have to learn to love ourselves

The funny thing about my relationship with my grandmother is that despite the hostilities that inevitably arise between us, the older I get, the more like her I become. I thought women were supposed to turn into their mothers as they age, but not me. I've skipped a generation and cut to the chase of acting like I'm eighty-six. It's not that I want to, it's that I can't help it. Maybe it's a biological connection, maybe just a subverted impulse to feign a biological connection. Regardless, I've weaseled my way into habits and circumstances so as to effortlessly mimic her behavior. I live alone and I own a laughable number of house plants. I've named them all after characters in my favorite romance novels—Thorfinn, Hazeltine, and Joceyln—and on lonely days, I talk to them. "Good morning!" I'll say. "Is Thorfinn thirsty? *I* think Thorfinn is thirsty!" I call myself fat, harass the mailman about lost catalogs, subsist largely on canned sardines. I eat most of my dinners alone while watching reruns of *Designing Women*. I'm confused by iPods.

Also, I'm an avid masturbator. I mention it because my grand-mother is also an avid masturbator. How do I know? My brother, Sam, told me. How does Sam know? He was with our neighbor Brian Epstein when Brian Epstein found her vibrator.

A BRIEF HISTORY OF MY PATH TOWARD AVID MASTURBATION

(My grandmother's history will follow and, in so doing, address the aforementioned vibrator.)

It all started with a young man named Randall Buckwald. I was a virgin until I was sixteen and, while I managed to learn the dis-tinction between an orgasm and impromptu urination before then, I was still convinced said orgasm would result from sex. But then I met Randall. And Randall changed everything. An aspiring dancer, he transferred to my high school from Minneapolis my junior year, and the first time I ever saw him, he was on the high school baseball diamond performing a series of ballet stretches. There he was, all five-feet four inches of him, outfitted in a leotard and tights to accentuate the musculature of his emaciated thighs. Well, lucky for me, I was born with a nose made for sniffing out potential partners—those lucky few who fall within the narrow confines of my league—so when I saw him, I thought, *He will have you. Make him yours.*

I accomplished the task easily enough through a series of cafe-teria lunches in which we sat side by side at an otherwise empty table. We discussed ballet, the virtues of Alanis Morissette, and what it was, exactly, that the letters *FUPA* stood for.

"This part here," I said, and flirtatiously placed Randall's hand atop my lower abdomen.

FUPA, for those unfamiliar with the term, is an acronym refer-ring to the bulge of a woman's gut that lies just above her pelvis. The non-emaciated, non–personally trained among us often have one. I had one. I *have* one. At my thinnest, mine looks like the faint beginnings of a baby bump; at my heaviest, like I've stuffed a living baby down my pants. One day in French class, my neighbor Brian Epstein said, "Yo, Barron! Nice FUPA!" to which our teacher, Madame Cohen, replied, *"En Français, s'il vous plaît!"*

So Brian said, *"Salut, Barron! Vous avez une FUPA trés belle!"*

Unsure if FUPA, as a noun, should be masculine or feminine, Madame Cohen asked Brian what it was. *"Qu'est-ce que c'est, FUPA?"* she asked.

"Fat Upper Pussy Area!" he answered.

Feminine, apparently.

I explained what FUPA meant, and Randall, seemingly comfortable to have his hand atop it, said, "Well, I like it, frankly. I think it's cute."

It was the sweetest thing he could have said, and I was smitten. If I had had my way, I would have tied a bow around his head and shrunk him down to troll-doll size so he'd fit neatly in my pocket, so we could be together always.

Companionship; a FUPA not just accepted, but adored. These were wonderful aspects of our courtship, but we still only lasted three months. Sex was the thing that eventually tore us apart. For Randall? Figuratively. For me? Literally. Randall may have been short, but he had feet as long as a baby and wide as a paperback book, and suffice it to say that at five foot four, when he disrobed, he looked like the front half of an elephant: two legs, one trunk. The sight might have struck another, more experienced woman as hitting the jackpot, but to me, it just looked suspicious. Intriguing, yes, but in much the same way I might find a handgun intriguing: It's new and different and so, of course, it piques my interest; but if I'm not careful, it'll kill me.

We were two months into our courtship when I finally agreed to try sex. *Try.* It was my way of saying thank you after he'd generously agreed to take me to see *Jerry Maguire* in a first-run movie theater. I'm easily aroused by men in formfitting bottoms (football players, cyclists, ballet dancers; this proclivity contributed to my initial attraction to Randall, I'm sure), and so the constant shots of Cuba Gooding Jr.'s peach-shaped rump convinced me to throw caution to the wind. But with disastrous results. Once we finally got down to business, Randall worked with alarming speed, exercising less control than an incontinent infant until I lost all feeling in my lower half and, eventually, control of my bladder. You'd think relieving yourself on another person's pubic hair would free you from the responsibility of having to have sex with him again, but no. Randall was sixteen and determined. He was not to be placated with bases one through three.

"Let's try it one more time," he'd plead. "Just once. I'll be quick, I swear."

"I know you will," I'd say, "but speed is not the issue. The issue is that now when I pee, it feels like a colony of fire ants have built a village in my crotch."

I thought my answer was wonderfully clever, but Randall disagreed. One month later he dumped me for a young woman named Lillian Freebaum. She was a five-foot-eleven-inch colossus of a dame, a high-school sophomore with hips of such impressive girth, they could've stopped traffic. (And more to the point, she harbored a vagina the size of a landfill.) It hurt to see him move along so quickly, but it also got the wheels turning: I'd learned real-life sex was about as much fun as a staph infection. Sure, I'd had a pee, but that was an action born from pain, not pleasure. And contrary to my opinions expressed in *The Porn,* sex didn't do much to alleviate the feelings that inspired me to write it in the first place. So what was I to do? Hungry people eat. Tired people sleep. And in a manner as instinctive, a young lady knocked on the head with the realization that sex with a panhandle of a unit incites a fear of death long before it does an orgasm, she intuits that what she ought to do is take matters into her own hands.

So that's what I did.

I masturbated so excessively for seven days that on the eighth I awoke to find my right hand paralyzed. Palsy-like. It was stuck in the pose one might strike to hold a grapefruit tight against her FUPA. Maybe this should've worried me, but it didn't: I knew *why* it was stuck, after all. And seeing as how every member of my family had their own electric toothbrush, I also knew that I had other options.

My mom was the one who got scared. She noticed me fumble my cereal spoon over breakfast.

"You're eating like a baby," she said. "What's wrong?"

My mother is a diagnosable hypochondriac who perceives any changes in her body or the bodies of those around her as the obvious onset of cancer or AIDS. Or maybe a stroke. In describing physical symptoms to her, you must choose your words carefully lest she fly off the handle and run you through a slew of biopsies and MRIs.

"I'm fine," I said. "My wrist just hurts a little."

"Move it."

"What?"

"Move your wrist. Move it around."

When I told her I couldn't, the color drained from her face. She ordered me into the car. "Why?" I asked, but she'd already turned away and run to the foot of the stairs so she could scream to my father, who was upstairs on the toilet, "I'M TAKING SARA TO THE HOSPITAL!"

My mother's never been good in a crisis, and my father's way of handling that has always been to prove he's worse. He stumbled toward the staircase with his pants around his ankles. "WHY?!" he screamed. "WHAT'S WRONG?!"

"STAY CALM!" she shouted back. "NOW PULL UP YOUR PANTS AND LISTEN CAREFULLY: SARA'S HAND IS FROZEN . . . *FOR NO APPARENT REASON!*"

I'm of the opinion that my father wasn't born a hypochondriac, but after thirty years of marriage to my mother, thirty years spent assessing a garden-variety headache as a rapidly expanding brain tumor, it's a mind-set he's absorbed. "OH, GOD!" he cried. "WHAT'S WRONG?!"

"I'M SURE SHE'S FINE!" she carried on. "I'M *SURE* SHE'S FINE. BUT SHE *COULD* HAVE HAD AN ANEURYSM AND I DON'T WANT TO RISK IT. WE'RE GOING TO THE HOSPITAL. YOU GET SAM TO SCHOOL!"

I hadn't had an aneurysm. That's what a dashing emergency-room internist by the name of Dr. Rasheedwa told me after running a series of tests at my mother's behest. "So now we've got to figure out what *is* wrong," he said afterward. "Have you done anything strenuous recently? Anything with that right hand? Anything out of the ordinary?"

Sporting my FUPA and saddlebag arms, I must have looked like the most likely candidate in the world for chronic masturbation. Dr. Rasheedwa *must have* known the score, but that didn't mean he'd want to talk about it. Not to me. Not to my mother. So he started throwing metaphoric bones. "Do you play tetherball?" he asked. "Or piano? Perhaps you do a lot of typing?"

"Yes!" I exclaimed. "Typing!" This option sounded plausible. "That *must* be it! I do a *lot* of typing!"

Dr. Rasheedwa nodded happily along and diagnosed me with carpal tunnel syndrome. Then he fit me for a wrist brace and told me to wear it for a month.

To quote my friend Jim, a morbidly obese aspiring opera singer I'd meet years later waiting tables—a young man who's never done well with the ladies and who, as a result, has mastered any and all nuances of "the craft," as he calls it, of self-gratification— "Once you go 'whack,' you never go back."

Once one knows *how* to masturbate, one *must* masturbate.

I, for one, could not agree more. If you, like me, didn't figure out masturbation until you were seventeen, the discovery was a revolutionary and spectacular gift. So to have it suddenly ripped away by a debilitating wrist brace? This was horribly traumatic, like giving a six-year-old a puppy, then shooting said puppy in the face. Awful. Unfair. And in some sorry twist of fate, my electric Oral-B went kaput later that same week, and my mother took her time replacing it. There *were* the others lying around of course, but using my parents' or my brother's struck even me as selfish and grotesque. Oh! And I'm not ambidextrous. My left hand is good at waving. And that's it.

Over the course of that next month in which I had to wear the wrist brace, I became so unimaginably irritable that my parents staged an intervention.

"You're so angry!" cried my dad. "Just talk to us! Please! Just tell us what's wrong!"

"Is it drugs?" my mother overlapped. "Pot? Something worse? Are you projecting your anger at Randall onto us?"

My mother has an amazing knack for wearing people down. She always has. She interrogates exhaustively to make the truth less daunting than the prospect of more questions. "Do you resent me for working when you were a child? Do you feel I withhold? Envy your brother? How are your grades? Has your father not loved you enough? Is this your way of distancing? Would you like to see a therapist yourself?"

"NO!" I finally cracked. "I CAN'T MASTURBATE WHEN I HAVE THIS WRIST BRACE ON, OKAY?" I brandished it at her. "*Jesus.* Just leave me *alone.*"

"Oh," said my dad.

"Well," said my mom.

We sat in awkward silence for a moment. We left it to my mom to be the one to break it.

"At least none of us have cancer," she said.

This much was true. Just a horribly awkward dinner ahead of us.

MY GRANDMOTHER'S AVID MASTURBATION
(A.k.a. The Vibrator)

So six years ago, my grandmother broke her hip. Unable to care for herself, she spent a month in a nursing home, over the course of which she called my mother six times a day. For thirty-one days. She'd need a new robe, different hand soap, Scotch tape. She'd be angry with a nurse or the limited food selection in the cafeteria. It was around day nineteen that the phone calls got my mother acting suicidal.

"I can't take it anymore," she'd say. "I can't go on. What's the point? I'm so tired."

My brother, Sam, had just arrived home from his freshman year at college, and he was the one to come to her rescue. She still had to answer all those phone calls, but the actual doing of the errands, the picking up and dropping off of sweaters, playing cards, extra-large bottles of Windex, this was all left up to Sam. He agreed because he was, at nineteen, deeply addicted to marijuana and so could stay mellow in the face of life's most aggravating aspects: patchouli oil, hemp jewelry, angry senior citizens. These were his "sure, whatever" years. Ask him a question, any question, and he'd tell you, "Sure, whatever."

Will you set the table? "Sure, whatever."

Mow the lawn? "Sure, whatever."

Take a twelve-pack of Ensure to Grandma at the nursing home? "Sure, whatever."

He was too stoned for anything to bother him.

One afternoon, our neighbor Brian Epstein spotted Sam as he was heading for the car and asked to join him on his errands. "Yo, bro!" he yelled across the yard. "Wassup? Where you goin'?"

Sam's older now. He kicked the pot addiction and few battle scars remain besides a half dozen Phish CDs and an unwavering allegiance to Tom's of Maine deodorant. So now he understands the importance of steering clear of suburban Caucasians who toss words like *bro* or *wassup* around; *now* he knows these types are good for nothing but a date-rape charge. But Sam wasn't always so wise. On this occasion, he let Brian come along.

"I have to pick up a twelve-pack of Ensure at my grandma's house and take it to her nursing home," he said.

"Can I come?" asked Brian. He knew marijuana would be on the itinerary.

"Sure," said Sam. "Whatever."

Brian Epstein is a young man whose talents begin and end with his knack for making other people uncomfortable (*see:* making reference to my FUPA in French class). It's what he does to get attention. So once he and Sam had successfully loaded the Ensure into the trunk of the car, Brian racked his brain to figure out what he could do to steer an otherwise pleasant afternoon horribly off course.

"Bro," he said, "before we go, we *got* to find your granny's dildo! You *know* she's got one! Grannies gotta jerk it, too!"

This is an awfully forward thing to say. But like I said, awful and forward are Brian Epstein's specialties.

Sam was thrown off guard and unsure how to answer at first. But given a second, he decided on no. "No, Brian," he said. "I do not want to find my grandma's dildo." But Brian ignored him and bounded up the stairs to our grandmother's bedroom. According to Sam, this was the point at which Brian started speaking in a whiny falsetto so as to effectively personify the imagined dildo's voice. "If I were a dildo, where would I be?" he trilled. "I bet I'd be near the bed so Grandma wouldn't have to walk too far to find me!" He inched toward her nightstand. "I bet I'd be in the nightstand!"

Then Brian reached into said nightstand and found a tube sock. He turned the tube sock upside down, and a vibrator fell out.

"Oh god," said Sam. "Why me?"

He may have been stoned and apathetic, but circumstances this dramatic warrant a reaction. Conversely, Brian was delighted. Flushed with joy and the adrenaline of having intuited correctly, he yelped with pride and grabbed the vibrator up off the floor.

"*En garde!*" he shouted. Like it was a sword. Brian entertained himself by chasing Sam around with it for a while until his mother texted to remind him that they had to be at synagogue by six.

"Gotta bounce," he said to Sam. "Let's head home and I'll holler at you later."

Sam and I find different aspects of this story wretched and surprising. Sam finds it wretched that he saw our grandma's vibrator. I find it wretched that Brian Epstein applies the verb *bounce* to his suburban person. Sam was surprised that our grandma owned a vibrator. I was surprised that owning said vibrator hadn't calmed

45

her down. And there was also a hopeful aspect I attached to the situation, which I think didn't resonate for Sam. I felt hopeful knowing a woman's body still wants a vibrator once she's over eighty. I may not be the most ambitious person in the world, but I've got goals, and that's one of them: I'd love to see my hot pocket keep popping for another sixty years. I was inspired by my grandmother's physical needs and desires. In fact, I admired them. I admired *her*. I'd swallow the fate of FM radio and canned sardines, I'd engage my plants in conversation and shoulder the burden of a solitude I fought with Delta Burke, if it meant I'd get to be like her once I got old.

Wow. I never thought I'd say that. But when masturbation's on the line, I guess I get a little crazy.

4

springtime

Like my dad, I've always enjoyed a steady routine. Had I a close-knit group of friends in school or some social organization I was enthused about—yearbook committee or chess club, say—perhaps my after-school habit would've been to catch a ride to the mall to "chill" with my "hens" in the food court. Maybe I would've logged countless hours shopping for backless tanks or scrunchy socks. But without the proper social structure to set such plans in motion, my routine instead involved a daily helping of *The Jerry Springer Show,* Monday through Friday from four to six P.M. The back-to-back episodes became the bright spot in my day and Jerry himself a god among men, a portal to endless, diverse slices of American life.

Jerry Springer gets a bad rap and I, for one, think that's unfair. All the criticism set upon the former mayor ignores the fact that for all his viewers stuck in a sea of self-pity, he's there in syndication to remind us that it could, in fact, be worse. Did I have a FUPA? Yes. A first cousin I'd screwed in '92? No. The occasional eczema flare-up?

Yes. A jail sentence for having raped my neighbor with a rolling pin? No. Jerry Springer helped me keep things in perspective.

One of the great things about D-list talk-show hosts is that they're more accessible than regular celebrities. Should you decide you want to see one in person, all you have to do is call the show's hotline. The invitation appears alongside a telephone number at each commercial break to ask: "Would you like to attend a live studio taping?"

Whenever this question arose, I'd seriously consider it. I'd imagine myself in the studio audience a mere thirty feet from the Springer guests du jour. I'd choose an aisle seat so that I might be picked to pose hard-hitting questions. "What possesses you?" I'd ask the foot fetishist or Baptist mission worker. "At what point did you decide, 'That's the thing for me'?"

Jerry would be impressed by my question. "That was good," he'd whisper in my ear as the show went to commercial. Then we'd chat for a moment about how much I enjoyed his work and *then*—having been blown away by my intelligence and poise— he'd offer me a job. Perhaps as his personal assistant? Or associate producer? I'd accept the offer regardless of the specified position, and with a five-figure income now forthcoming, I'd get to skip college. I'd cut straight to my role as Self-Sufficient Modern Gal. Not girl. *Gal:* Kicky. Fun. Fresh. I'd live in a bachelorette pad with a Jacuzzi and a canopy bed.

Would I like to attend a live *Jerry Springer* taping?

"Why, yes," I decided. "Yes. I think I would."

Like Ferris Bueller in the eponymous film, I thought I deserved a day off from school, and an afternoon at the Springer studios sounded like the perfect way to spend it. We shared a goal of escape, Ferris and I, but pursued our dreams differently: He drove a Ferrari and I, a Ford Escort station wagon. And instead of bringing my wealthy best friend and attractive significant other along for the ride, I brought Ishmael Applebaum, a homosexual I'd befriended in my high-school acting class. The "chick with a dick" debacle of '91 had soured me on swimsuits and humanity, but not acting. I still wanted desperately to be onstage and so took acting classes all through high school, studying subjects as diverse as mime and trust falls. Ishmael and I got friendly during the trust-fall lesson, as we were both too big to want to do one.

"I absolutely refuse," he'd said.

Our acting teacher Professor Edelman, a woman who'd received a master's degree and called herself "professor" despite teaching acting at the high-school level, had moronically paired Ishmael with a decrepit anorexic named Sally. It would be feeble Sally's job to catch portly Ishmael, and Ishmael wasn't having it.

"But I *don't* trust her to catch me," he explained, "and I don't need a fall to tell me so."

"Well, *I* don't need the negative attitude," said Professor Edelman. "I'm going to have to ask you to sit outside for the remainder of the period."

"Thank *god*," he said. And then with great fanfare he tossed this gorgeous linen scarf around his neck, picked up his handbag, and paraded toward the door.

I wanted a piece of his action. Platonically. I raised my hand. "You know," I said, "I'm actually not comfortable with trust falls, either."

"WELL, THEN FINE!" she screamed. Ishmael's saucy attitude had lit her fuse, and she was primed to have me send her flying off the handle. "THEN THERE'S THE DOOR!"

I walked outside and slouched against the wall beside Ishmael.

"You, too?" he asked.

"Me, too," I said. "I hate trust falls, too."

He nodded. "They're simply unwise for anorexics and fat people. I'm sorry, but they are."

Ishmael was exactly the kind of guy who'd know this sort of thing. He was a self-described "successful child actor," and over the course of the years I'd spent busying myself with middle- and high-school musical productions, he'd been out there living the dream. He'd appeared in a *Sesame Street* knockoff on PBS singing a song about palindromes, and also on one of our local cable channels in a commercial for scuba gear. I was deeply jealous but also inspired, and these feelings, plus our similarly zaftig figures, built the foundation of our friendship.

Also, Ishmael Applebaum loved Jerry Springer. One spring afternoon he had an audition in downtown Chicago for a holiday revue starring Sandy Duncan called *That's Christmas!* and I decided to join him. We thought we'd make a day of it: Sara and Ishmael's Day Off. Audition in the morning, *Springer* in the afternoon. Ishmael's mother agreed since he'd be missing school anyway for his *That's Christmas!* audition, and my mom agreed because she was thrilled to see I'd made a friend and she wanted to encourage me. And also because she loves Sandy Duncan's glass eye. One of my mother's favorite pastimes is observing people with glass eyes and guessing which one's glass; as a result, Sandy Duncan has always been her ideal celebrity sighting. She agreed to call me out of school as long as I fetched her an autograph.

"And when you do," she said, "watch her eyes. See—get it? 'See'! Ha-ha!—if you can't pick out the glass one."

The sad news was that I couldn't get an autograph because Sandy Duncan wasn't even at the audition, and Ishmael didn't get a callback. They had him sing a song called "Cool Yule!" that was out of his baritone range, then told him he was free to go. The good news was that his immediate dismissal meant we arrived early to the *Jerry Springer* studio and reserved our place at the front of the line for ticket distribution and seat selection. We stood waiting behind the other early birds, two men named Darryl and Don. Darryl passed the time drinking from a brown paper bag, while Don did all the talking. He carried on about "those Bears!" "those Bulls!" and a woman he knew from college named Sheila who had a "tight pussy, man! Tight! Like an a-hole!" How it was that Don deemed the word *asshole* more offensive than a public mention of a pussy and its noteworthy level of tightness was beyond me. But to each his own. And at least his monologue made the wait go faster.

It took three hours from the time Ishmael and I arrived outside the studio to when I finally saw my Jerry in the flesh: two hours standing in line, one half hour choosing seats, one half hour enduring the show's warm-up act, a comedian named Laffz. All of Laffz's jokes centered around the concept of "dropping a deuce" and checking the toilet after he'd done so. He peppered his routine with phrases like "where my boyz at?!" and "holla!" and once he finally finished, explained how we, the audience, were expected to behave once Jerry got onstage. "I'm about to bring Jerry out, y'all," he said, "and when I do, y'all gotta *scream*! Be like, 'Jerry! Jerry! Jerry!' till I give the cue to stop!"

As instructed, we went wild once Jerry arrived. Most people chanted his name, but the gentleman seated directly behind me chose instead to belch it syllable for syllable. This delighted his companion, a young woman who, aside from the T-shirt she wore that read ONLY FUCK ME IF YOU LOVE ME, looked like the missing evolutionary link between me and my ancient monkey cousins. She and I were the same size with identical coloring, but she'd traded in my FUPA for a set of buck teeth that could've chucked wood and a forehead the size of a frying pan.

"That girl looks just like you!" squealed Ishmael. I glared at him the way you'd glare at someone who's just said you look like a Neanderthal. "Oh, you know what I mean," he backpedaled. "It's just that you both have red hair."

I loathe this as a follow-up to drawing undesirable physical parallels. I've been told I look like a redhead with massive facial scarring and, on a separate occasion, a redheaded transsexual. Male-to-female, but still: I'm always offended. And when I give a look that says so, the offending party always references the hair.

"Oh, you know what I mean!"

"Yes. I do. You think I look transsexual."

"No no *no*! It's just the hair. It's just that you both have red hair!"

Well, I had *not* come to a live *Springer* show taping to be made to feel bad about myself. I'd come for the entertainment, for the forthcoming guest who'd likely address her fiancé about having screwed her mom. I'd come for my daily helping of perspective. I

51

huffed at Ishmael and turned my focus back to Jerry, who thanked us for the warm reception and told us to prepare for a "wild ride!"

"This show is about people who keep their scandalous jobs a secret from their loved ones," he explained, "so hold on to your hats! Who knows what'll happen?!"

What happened was that a stripper named Pussytilt came to the stage with her boyfriend, Will, in tow. Pussytilt told Will it was time he learned what she really did for a living. "I don't work customer service at Walgreens like I said I did," she confessed. That's when a rush of music blasted through the studio speakers and Pussytilt grabbed a random man from the audience. She brought him to the stage, shoved him in a chair, and asked if he was ready to be "rocked." "PUSSYTILT'S GONNA ROCK YOU," she bellowed. "YOU READY?"

You could tell Will was uncomfortable with the whole situation and I felt bad for him. But Ishmael made a good point. "I'm sorry," he'd said, "but when someone goes by 'Pussytilt,' she's probably not the customer service representative she claims to be. As far as I'm concerned, *you're* the asshole if you're surprised once Pussytilt starts pussy tilting."

Anyway, there was a lot of aggressive shimmying and pelvic thrusts and this intricate swinging of her breasts that I found impressive. But Will, again, just looked uncomfortable. "You goddamn slut," he murmured. "You fucking slut."

Usually I'm quick to ramble on about the double standards inherent in a slur like *slut,* which has no real male equivalent, and so condemns a person not just for promiscuity, but for the simple act of being female. But once you start swatting your pierced nipples at a stranger's face in front of your boyfriend on national TV? Well, then I'm forced down off my high horse. I thought Will had made a decent point. Pussytilt, however, disagreed.

"I'M NOT A SLUT!" she shouted back, and then she ran her hand along the side of her body as though to encourage a perusal of her goods. "IF YOU CAN'T HANDLE ALL THIS . . ." What?

Pubescent physique? Enviable career? "Then *you* the pussy, Will! YOU THE PUSSY!"

I don't remember who swung first, but once the *pussy* bomb dropped, the two became a violent, whirling mass of nipple rings and graying teeth. Jerry's security men escorted them offstage as Jerry ushered in the next couple. He introduced them as Jamal and Majesty, and then explained that Jamal was not the everyday plumber he had claimed to be.

"What's different about you?" prompted Jerry.

"How about if I show you?" asked Jamal.

Jerry nodded excitedly and told Jamal to "take it away."

Jamal, like Pussytilt, brought a random audience member up onto the stage, except he chose a woman instead of a man. He disrobed, squeezed a packet of ketchup onto his G-string, and instructed the stranger to lick it off. Then he rewarded her with a single long-stemmed yellow rose. Jerry summed the act up nicely when afterward he said, "So you're a plumber, but also an exotic dancer? Is that the idea?"

Jamal nodded. "Uh-huh," he said, still out of breath. "I get hired out for birthdays mostly to earn extra cash."

"And what do you have to say to Majesty about all this?"

Majesty had taken to sobbing noiselessly in her chair. Jamal walked over and kneeled before her. "I've been saving money, Majesty, so I could buy you this." And then from the pocket of his discarded overalls he pulled a tiny felt box. Jamal explained that this was where the extra cash had gone. Everyone in the audience let out a collective "Aww." Everyone, that is, except Ishmael. "A diamond isn't apology enough for wearing a thong," he said. "In *public*."

But Majesty felt differently. She shrieked with delight and referred to her ring as "bomb-ass."

The only person unmoved by the engagement besides Ishmael was the red-haired Neanderthal behind me. "That Majesty is stoo-pid," she kept saying to her boyfriend. "How come *she* gets to get married?"

I listened but did not indulge in this sort of catty, competitive behavior. I may not have had a boyfriend. I may have had only Ishmael, who, while pleasant company, did not desire me physically. (Fueled by a number of illegally consumed Zimas and inspired by Randall Buckwald's awesome persistence several months before, there *was* this one Friday night in which I suggested Ishmael and I try taking things to the "next level." But when I offered, he declined. "Sara," he said gently, "how appealing would it be to you to kiss, let's say, your neighbor's dog." My neighbors didn't have a dog, and I made this point to Ishmael. "Well, I guess what I'm trying to say is that you're not attracted to dogs. That's my point. So you're not going to want to kiss one.") I may have been a dog in *my* man's metaphor. I may have been preying on the misfortune of others in a manner more grotesque than licking ketchup off a G-string, but at least I didn't ever say *bomb-ass*. And at least I, unlike Neanderthal, tried to let this speck of superiority mitigate my more primal jealous instincts.

Jerry rounded out the hour with a father-son duo named Lucky and Rusty. Rusty was there to tell his father, Lucky, he was gay and he'd dropped out of school to work as a go-go dancer. Lest Lucky find this information difficult to process, Rusty had brought his friend, another male go-go dancer, along to help demonstrate. This gent pranced onstage to the dance-remix version of "I'll Make Love to You" by Boyz II Men, then he and Rusty mimed a wide array of graphic sexual activities.

"Who knew 'making love' involved a rim job?" asked Ishmael.

"Rusty," I answered. "Rusty knew."

Lucky watched the performance, called his son a "faggot," and stormed offstage. The word *faggot* offended the other go-go dancer, who shouted back, "You're probably a faggot yourself, faggot, if watchin' us dance makes you so angry."

"No, he *didn't*," said Neanderthal, "that go-go fag did *not* just say that shit to the daddy!"

But he did.

Lucky charged back onstage and pummeled the go-go dancer's

face into the armrests of his chair until the security guards broke them apart and dragged them away.

"This brings me to my final thought," said Jerry.

At the end of every *Springer* show, my Jerry does a bit called "Final Thought." Here, he ruminates on the theme of that day's show. And on this particular day, the theme was honesty. "Why do we choose to keep secrets from those we love?" he asked. "Why do we build up walls with lies?"

"Why does Rusty have a boyfriend?" asked Ishmael. "*I* don't have a boyfriend."

"Rusty also mimes rim jobs in front of his dad," I answered. "I think you're the one who's better off."

We left the studio and drove home, mostly in silence. It was weird. In my imagined version of "Sara and Ishmael's Day Off" our drive home was filled with laughter and enlivened recollections of the day's events, but in reality we sat comatose, like we'd binged on a pile of lard; like how lard is delicious baked into a cookie, but grotesque if sucked down on its own, Jerry's guests are spectacular filtered through a camera, but watching them live starts to hurt. It's just too much. You don't notice at first because you're distracted by the man belching "Jer-ry, Jer-ry, Jer-ry" in your ear, but when you're driving home in your parents' Ford Escort station wagon with nothing so enchanting to distract you, what once was funny (pussy tilting) gets depressing. It's quiet; you're reflective. You realize there's been nothing ironic in your love of *Jerry Springer:* You drove downtown, you stood in line, you made an effort and enjoyed it, entertained as you were by the thinly veiled misery of someone else. That's the root of *your* perspective.

This realization made me wonder if perhaps I shouldn't try to kick my *Springer* habit altogether. I could do it cold turkey. But then I realized such a routine would mean missing the chance to see myself on-screen once the episode aired. And that, clearly, was too big a price to pay for any sort of moral rectitude.

Several months later I was lying on my couch per my usual routine to watch *The Jerry Springer Show* when Jerry announced something about scandalous jobs kept secret from loved ones. I sat up expectantly and sure enough, there was Jamal in his ketchup-stained zebra-print thong. And there, surprisingly, was I. It was just what I'd been waiting for: the two-foot version of my face, eyeing the ketchup-stained zebra-print thong.

I figured that that would be it, that now I could relax into the remainder of the episode. But as it turned out, this was the first of five appearances—*five*—I'd make over the course of the episode. The show's editors used me in every available reaction shot. Pussytilt strips, cut to Sara, Sara gasps! Jamal doles out a yellow rose, cut to Sara, Sara gasps! And so on. They seemed to adore how overtly responsive I was, and this came as a pleasant surprise seeing as how it's a quality for which I'm often criticized. Family and friends find it "annoying"; they think it's "exhausting" that, where someone else sees fit to roll her eyes—lost keys—I see fit to sob. Or that where someone else might sob—a breakup—I see fit to manipulate with threats of drug addiction. Apparently, these antics tire people out.

But not TV producers; these shenanigans are right up their alley. In addition to my five—*five!*—appearances on the actual episode, I also snagged a spot on that week's *Talk Soup and* on the first-ever *Jerry Springer Too Hot for TV* video. I appear toward the end, laughing hysterically when the Boyz II Men hit "I'll Make Love to You" comes on.

I'd been immortalized on-screen and I felt proud. Any sense of *Jerry Springer* disaffection went away, covered up as it was by the flush of adrenaline that accompanies attention. It's a dangerous affection, one that paves the way for other entertaining bouts of degradation and puts you on par with, let's say, an aspiring go-go dancer who feigns oral sex in front of his dad. Lives of quiet desperation are saved for other types with other problems: repressers, avoiders; I envision a Nebraskan mailman who can't force himself to say "I love you." Well, we attention hounds live lives of equal desperation, it's just that ours get sported on a sleeve. For your entertainment. It's our way of giving back, we kid ourselves, and book the flight to either coast to stumble, crash, and burn.

urbia

5

big girl on campus

I moved to New York City when I was eighteen. My attitude prior to living here is best expressed by Libby Mae Brown, Parker Posey's character in the 1996 homage to community theater *Waiting for Guffman*. "New York is an island," she says, "is really what it is. It's this island full of people of different colors and ideas. It sounds like a lot of fun to me. I'd like to maybe meet some guys—Italian guys!—and, you know, watch TV and stuff." I, too, pictured a condensed landmass of attractive men of various ethnicities. I pictured them perched on the stoops of picturesque brownstones. I imagined they'd have impressive musculature, and I a myriad of professional acting auditions to attend.

I was accepted as a drama major at a downtown Manhattan university after performing with a Cockney accent two minutes' worth of original poetry. How, you ask, or why? Because people make mistakes; an admissions officer forgets her morning coffee, and BOOM! Just like that, the wrong person get admitted. Sam's current girlfriend went to Harvard and she references *Maid in Manhattan* as her favorite movie. "It rocks!" she'll say. And she's not kidding. Apply the transitive property (if A=B and B=C, then A=C) to determine that the less-than-brightest bulbs *can* get into Harvard. People slip through the cracks. Good for us, bad for them. Bad for a prestigious place like Harvard that their alumnae offer nonironic praise to *Maid in Manhattan*. Have you seen it? You should. It'll make you feel good about yourself and *your* accomplishments.

There's a lot of talk in acting circles of a willingness to "go there." I never knew for sure what that meant, but now, years later and after having studied the Craft, I've decided it relates to one's level of self-awareness, an abandonment of self-consciousness coupled with an inversely proportional amount of self-absorption. It's a tricky combination, a complex talent, unique to gifted actors and diagnosable psychotics. And to my auditioner, I, lightly mustachioed and bellowing lines of tenth-rate prose, must have seemed capable of either extreme. So they took a chance and let me in. That, and my parents could afford the full tuition, and an admissions office loves that in a student; they rank it higher than something as subjective as, say, talent.

I moved into my dorm room in the fall of 1997 and my first night there, I met my roommates, Peg and Maude.

"Hi!" I said excitedly. "I'm Sara Barron, your new roommate!"

Peg, too busy unpacking her array of Hello Kitty paraphernalia, ignored me completely, but Maude was more forthcoming. "Hey," she said, "wanna shot? There's Jäger in the minifridge."

I don't much like doing shots. They make me sick. I can eat gefilte fish or organ meats, no problem. But if I consume hard liquor quickly, I'll be toilet-bound for *hours*. It's a lesson learned the hard way. Here, I shot the Jäger, got the spins, then spent the next hour in the bathroom as my roommates made executive decisions on everything from bed selection to wall decor. When I emerged, three Hello Kitty posters hung on the wall alongside a crucifix. The Jesus seemed to mock me. "Don't drink the liquor of my people," I swear I heard him say. "You, *Jew,* can't handle it."

Peg and Maude were best friends from high school who'd requested to live together. Their friendship, they'd explain, was Deep. They'd tell me, "Our connection is beyond words," and instead express their allegiance through coordinating outfits and tattoos. On the day we met, both donned matching T-shirts known as "baby Ts." Baby Ts are T-shirts sized to fit babies; they're *sized* to fit babies, but full-grown women like to wear them instead. Peg and Maude wore baby Ts with cerulean backgrounds and fuchsia lettering. Peg's asked GOT MILK? while Maude's declared, BLONDES MAY HAVE MORE FUN, BUT BRUNETTES GET THE JOB DONE!

What job? I thought. *Spreadsheets? Filing? Is it something more risqué?*

Peg's message, thank god, was easier to decipher. ("Got milk"! On breasts! 'Cause breasts "got milk." Get it?!)

Peg and Maude were very clever.

Their tattoos matched, too: large radiant suns on their lower backs with thoughtful annotations etched along the borders. Peg's said, DO UNTO OTHERS AS YOU'D HAVE THEM DO UNTO YOU, and Maude's, WORK HARD, PLAY HARDER.

I once saw a comedian do a routine about women with tattoos on their lower backs. "Know what I call 'em?" he'd asked. "Doggy-style decorations!"

There was the punch line. Next, the overexplanation.

"Since when you turn your girl over to do her like a dog, you got something fun to look at!" One man in the audience laughed. He had on a cowboy hat. "And it's always some *Laura Ashley* shit, you know? Like a rose or some shit. Which is weird since these girls are always—and I'm sorry to say it—sluts! But they are!"

Highbrow it wasn't, but it made a good point. A lower-back tattoo, when outlined in philosophies of karmic justice and paired with baby T and visible thong, is the mark of a promiscuous woman. The proof is in the pudding: *My* lower back bears nothing but a half dozen moles and a string of errant hairs, and at eighteen I was lucky to get a biennial hand down the pants. Peg Pearson, on the other hand, a woman *with* a lower-back tattoo, had a rotating roster of beaus, an hombre a week she'd entertain with the self-titled "Peggy Pearson Sexy Special." It was a performance lasting thirty minutes, and provided you had alcohol and penis on hand, you qualified as an eligible partner.

Here was the arc to her performance: Peggy and her chosen gent would walk through the front door to our bedroom. "Make yourself comfortable," she'd say, and whoever he was, he'd head to the bathroom to either urinate or vomit. Sometimes both. Then Peggy would disrobe. Now outfitted only in a thong (MADE YOU LOOK! said the set of seven, the letters crammed on the inch of fabric streched across her pubic bone), she'd saunter toward her stereo to play the Shania Twain song "You're Still the One."

"You're Still the One" is a melodic ballad about a couple whose relationship grows stronger with every passing year. It's an odd romantic sentiment to hear juxtaposed against belligerent, teenage, midcoital shouts:

"*You're still the one . . .*"

"Is that my pussy?!"

"*. . . The only one I dream of . . .*"

"You like my pussy?!"

"*You're still the one I kiss goodniiiiiiight . . .*"

"SAY YOU LIKE TO FUCK MY PUSSY!"

Before meeting Peg, I'd rarely heard the word *pussy* used in reference to anything besides a stripper who was tilting. Basically, I thought it meant a baby cat. "You like my pussy?" and "Say you like to fuck my pussy" weren't words I realized got exchanged between people. And despite how resentful I eventually became of Peg's loud and disruptive behavior, so must I credit her for expanding my horizons. People (men specifically, as has been my hetero experience) like to say graphic things behind closed doors; they like to ask personal questions, and not "What's your relationship like with your mother?" And had I not lived with Peggy Pearson, had I not memorized her repertoire word for dirty word, then I'd have missed the chance to learn how a lady should respond.

While Peg was a dirty girl figuratively, Maude was literally dirty. She shirked traditional cleaning methods—toothpaste and showers weren't of interest—grooming instead with a nail clipper. She'd spend her evenings clipping her nails, then tossing the remnants on the floor between our beds. One morning I awoke to find one in my mouth. I called my mother to ask her what to do.

"WHAT DO YOU DO?!" she screamed back. "You confront! That's what! You be direct! You tell that girl that your mother's not spending eight hundred dollars a month on housing so *you* can eat toenails! What a fucking slob!" I heard my father in the background correct her language. "I'LL SAY *FUCKING* IF I WANT TO SAY *FUCKING*!" she wailed. "THE GIRL WITH THE CRUCIFIX CLIPS HER TOENAILS AND THEN THROWS THEM ON THE FLOOR! AND TODAY YOUR DAUGHTER ATE ONE!"

I took my mother's advice and addressed the situation head-on. I tried to be mature. Direct. I said, "Maude, I woke up the other morning and one of your toenails was in my mouth. I found that sort of disconcerting. Could you try throwing them out in the garbage from now on?"

Maude rolled her eyes. "We'll see," she said, then walked to the minifridge, shot a quarter cup of Jäger, and placed a sanitary pad in her red Jockey thong.

That was the other thing about Maude. With the regularity that someone else would brush her teeth, Maude wore a sanitary pad. Every day: thong, socks, sanitary pad. What necessitated the daily self-diaperings? Bladder problems? Frequent bleeding? I never knew for sure and was only privy to the situation because she'd don the pads in public. In our bedroom. Right in front of Peg and me.

I understand that all roommates, whether a stranger at eighteen or a spouse at forty-five, are destined to annoy you. I understand that *I'm* annoying: I'm passive-aggressive, mean to pets, adept at double standards. I've been told, "You snore so loud, I hate you." I understand it's no walk in the park to live with me either, but, simply stated, Peg and Maude were worse. Sanitary pads, nail shards, Shania Twain. It's more than one woman should ever have to handle.

Someone else would have filled out the paperwork necessary to request a room change, but paperwork's too high on my list of earth-shattering fears: 1) dying alone, 2) tapeworms, 3) paperwork. I knew there'd be an inch-high stack if I wanted new roommates, and frankly, that potential scared me more than another day spent privy to Peg's eponymous "Special." I mean, I'd sort of gotten used to it by the end of first semester, accepting the questions posed about her "pussy" as my own urban lullaby.

When I wasn't in my dorm room, I kept busy with my acting. As a drama major, I took classes in speech and movement. These were subjects in which I'd previously thought myself to be well versed, but it turned out: No, I wasn't. I spoke well enough for a normal person, sure, but not for an actor. Actors had to study.

My movement teacher, an angry woman named Judy, built a lesson plan around her drum. She was similar to Ms. Manishevitz, my junior high school acting teacher, but with several key differences: Judy used kettledrums native to Jamaica in lieu of Ms. Manishevitz's old standby, the congas. And Judy came with a price tag of $5,000 a semester.

Twice a week in movement class the students were told to march across the movement studio one at a time as Judy struck her drum and shouted the names of animals or emotions: "Bird!" "Angry!" "Elk!" "Confused!" Then it was our job to convey that animal or emotion on our walk across the floor.

When a woman with a kettledrum who wears a mauve beret barks at me to be an elk, I find it hard to muster much enthusiasm. This made Judy angry.

"You!" she'd shout. "In the tights! What do you think *you're* doing?"

If that wasn't the million-dollar question. What *was* I doing? Where was the audience? The applause? I'd been hoping for my own musical accompanist. "Hit it, buster!" I'd imagined saying to a swarthy, six-foot piano man. And then Buster would bang out

"Macavity the Mystery Cat" from *Cats* as I joined him in a throaty, Piaf-inspired rendition, to the delight of my peers and instructors. Cawing like an elk while outfitted in leotard, tights, and extraneously worn jazz shoes fell tragically short of these expectations; that was the god's honest truth. But a white woman pounding a kettledrum most likely can't handle the truth. So I started faking it.

"ELK! ELK! ELK!" I'd cry brightly every time I crossed the dance floor. This way I'd avoid Judy's line of fire. And at the time, my dignity seemed a small price to pay to help hold her together.

On our days off from the kettledrum, Judy instructed us on something called the Alexander Technique. Google "Alexander Technique" and you'll learn it's an established method of improving breath and posture. Those are lessons worth learning as an actor, but Judy's instruction went like this: "Lie on the floor. Picture your spine getting longer. Go." And then we'd have the remaining hour of class in which to do so.

All I learned from this was how to fall asleep on hardwood floors. As for the other students, I can't speak for them, obviously, but I *can* say that my morning naps were often interrupted by their snoring. Oh! And that no one's posture and/or breath support improved for shit.

Judy's class was in the morning. In the afternoon, I'd study voice with an aging homosexual named Whitfield. Here's what he taught me:

> *Two toads who were terribly tired went trotting along the road. Said toad number one to toad number two, "It's hot and I carry a load."*

It's a poem. Whitfield told me to recite it a hundred times a day to help improve my diction. I'd do as instructed in the evenings while Maude was busy clipping.

"What the *fuck*?" she'd shout over my nightly recitations. "*Stop!* You sound possessed."

65

It was a fair point. I must have sounded—what?—troubled; I must have sounded *very* troubled. But once you eat another person's nail clippings, and once you're refused an apology for said offense, you find it difficult to care what she thinks when she hears you talking to yourself about "toads" and their respective "loads" for hours at a time.

"Maude," I'd say, "shut up. I'm practicing my Craft."

"Oh, whatever!" she'd shoot back. "You're a psycho!"

"No," I'd answer, "I'm an Actor. There's a difference."

Every day in class, Whitfield wore a dickey. Do you know what a dickey is? I didn't. Not until my voice teacher wore one, anyway, and declared, "My! I'm sweating in my dickey!"

A dickey is the top of a turtleneck, a turtleneck if you cut it just below the collar. You wear one underneath a sweater for example, for the *illusion* of a turtleneck—the turtleneck *line,* if you will—without the accompanying heat. They were all the rage in 1984 but by '97 had fallen to the wayside for everyone who wasn't homosexual. Whitfield wore one every day with a pullover sweater and pashmina scarf.

I, for one, am inclined to associate a man bedecked in dickey and pashmina with a certain amount of sensitivity; a gentleman wears a pashmina in eggshell, and I'm expecting to get coddled. But that wasn't Whitfield's style. The third week of class, he told us all to choose a poem to recite for our fellow students. Some went highbrow: Wordsworth, Yeats. Some went Beat: Ginsburg. Some (an ambitious young spitfire by the name of Sara Barron) forgot the assignment entirely and so had to fly by the seat of her pants. Lucky for her, she'd memorized her fair share of verse over the years.

"One fish, two fish," I announced, "red fish, blue fish."

My audience looked unimpressed. Whitfield picked at a hangnail. "You," he said, "are very bad."

I tried not to take it personally. This sort of harsh approach was typical. An obese girl named Gloria had gone before me with a sonnet. "How do I love thee?" she'd begun, but was quickly interrupted.

"STOP!" cried Whitfield. "Please *stop*! A love poem from a fat girl is simply *too* depressing. Try again tomorrow with something more upbeat."

And to an effeminate fellow named Serge who literally put the class to sleep with a singsong version of "The Raven," he'd said only, "Oh *god,* no! Serge, my darling, I'm sorry to have to be the one to tell you, but you swish louder than Gloria's pantyhose."

The problem with acting teachers is that they tend—*tend*—to be embittered. Reality crushed their unrealistic ambitions years ago, so they settled on teaching. They picked up the pieces of their shattered dreams and hightailed it to an acting school to earn a paycheck at the expense of the next generation of delusionists. To be fair, I must acknowledge this as *my* rule based on *my* experience; I'm aware there are exceptions to it. I accept that some people genuinely want to teach acting and that, as a result, they have some talent for it. I can believe that those people are out there. I can also believe there's a clan of olive green midgets on Mars who all wear matching twinsets. Why? Because it's what my grandfather told me after his stroke, just days before he died. I'll take a leap of faith and believe in a crew of intergalactic midgets or a contented acting teacher if that's what's asked of me. But I sure as Sherlock haven't ever seen one in the flesh. And I sure as Sherlock don't plan to hold my breath.

When asked by my father what I was learning at college, I was hard-pressed to answer honestly. I could've said, "I learned how to masturbate in my top bunk without moving," but I thought such forthrightness might upset him. Instead, I opted for quasi-honest with a hefty splash of unspecific.

"Well," I'd say from a street-side pay phone. Peggy was always in our dorm room having sex. I didn't care to have it underscore my conversation. "I took an improv class today."

"Oh! Improvisation!" he screamed over the *Rent* soundtrack blaring in the background. The double box set had been his birthday present from my mother. "Improv is such fun! You never know what'll happen! It's such an adventure!"

I associate the word *adventure* with a pirate or a talking horse. Not an improv class taught by an elderly paraplegic who rubs the stubs of his legs to keep himself awake.

"Well, not really an adventure so much as—"

"Sweetheart," he interrupted, "your mother's giving me the 'Watch the long-distance bill' look. We'd better wrap it up."

I could hear a scuffle for the phone. My mother won. "Honey, I'm sorry but we really have to go. Give a call back when you figure out what all this acting crap—"

"Lynn, please!" I heard my father scold.

"Oh, all right," she huffed. "Fine. I'm sorry. What all this acting . . . technique is good for."

My improv teacher's name was Marvin Zlotnick, and he was eighty-five and a paraplegic. No one knew where his legs were, and no one knew why he was qualified to teach. His instruction sounded like the ramblings of a homeless schizophrenic: "You and you! Go play there. Now, I said. NOW! What?! Who knows, I'm tired. Where's my water?"

For all his senility, Marvin still managed to teach me the core tenet of improvisation: saying "yes, and . . ." When your scene partner asks, for example, "Is that your stick of butter?" you say, "Yes, and . . . might you like a patty?" etc. It's the phrase that keeps a scene afloat. It's how you keep it going. I'd be improvising about a vacuum cleaner or a Cantonese babysitter when Marvin, tired, legless, moody, and confused, would awaken from a nap shouting, "Yes, and! Say it *NOW*!"

For example:

"Tseng-Yi, did you let little Timmy watch TV?"

"I sorry, lady, please . . ."

Marvin snaps awake, rubs his stubs. "Yes, and! Say it *NOW*!"

"Yes, and . . . I feed him big cookie, too! Ha-ha!"

On the last Friday of the month, the acting school would put on a showcase performed by the students, for the students. People would sing (Peggy Lee's "Fever" was a staple, performed, more often than not, in a boa and/or arm-length gloves), enact two-person scenes (*Angels in America,* sans boa and/or arm-length gloves, also a staple), or improvise based on audience suggestions. I'm lazy, yes, but not when there's attention/applause on the line, so I managed to pull together a different act for every show. September: poetry reading. October: Shakespearean monologue. November: African dance routine. December: my own rendition of Nina Simone's "Mississippi Goddam." See the pattern? My aesthetic becomes more culturally "sensitive" as the semester wears on. This was due to the fact that in early November, I developed a wretched crush on a mini Denzel in my improv class named Elijah. And performing "black" material was how I thought I'd woo him.

I invited Peggy Pearson with me to the December showcase. By the end of first semester we'd gotten friendlier, due in large part to her dramatic weight gain. Between early September and late December Peggy Pearson packed on thirty pounds thanks to the vicious cycle of diet and exercise she seemed incapable of breaking. She gained weight from the buffet of trans fats in the dorm cafeteria and therefore had significantly less sex, and sex had been her only cardio.

"I'm fat," she'd said one night. "What should I do?"

"Lay off the cheesesteaks?" I suggested. "Try a step class?"

"Nooooo," she whined. "I mean, what should I do *tonight*? I'm bored."

My snazzy ensemble—African head scarf paired with corduroy overalls—must have suggested that I had somewhere else to be. And I could tell that Peggy craved an invite.

"Well, I *am* doing a performance of 'Mississippi Goddam' at my acting school tonight," I said. "You can come with me if you want."

I'd started feeling bad for Peg. For one thing, no one understood as well as I the effects of a FUPA on a sex life. And what was more, her friendship with Maude seemed to be suffering now that they lived together.

"The sanitary pads are *a problem*," Peg whispered one November night while Maude was in the bathroom. "And the nail clipping's worse."

"Preaching to the choir," I responded. "I ate one yesterday."

Peg looked at me, disgusted. "A toenail," I clarified, "not a sanitary pad."

Later that night, Peg sat watching the aforementioned "Fever" rendition, followed by a pas de deux to TLC's "Waterfalls" before I, in head scarf, took the stage.

"HELLO," I boomed. I'd learned in voice class to do something called "project." "MY NAME IS SARA BARRON AND I'D LIKE TO SING A SONG FOR YOU CALLED 'MISSISSIPPI GODDAM.'" In the fantasized version of this scenario, my musical accompanist, Buster, would bang out a few chords to get the number rolling, but here, I had to go a cappella.

"ALABAMA'S GOTTEN ME SO UPSET," I sang. "TENNESSEE MADE ME LOSE MY REST, AND EVERYBODY KNOWS ABOUT MISSISSIPPI GODDAM! *GODDAM!*"

Peggy had been sitting in the back of the black-box theater over the course of my performance, and when I joined her afterward, she didn't seem to want to look me in the eye. She kept her focus on her FUPA.

"Earth to Peggy!" I yelled, having sat down beside her. "Come *in,* Peggy! What'd you think?! Did you like it? Did you see that tall drink of chocolate in the second row? His name is Elijah. Could you tell if *he* liked it?"

Social graces weren't Peg's strong suit. This was evidenced by the devil-may-care attitude inherent in her "Sexy Special," and also here, when she said, "Well, I guess I ought to tell you not to quit your day job. Isn't that what people say?"

"But I don't have a day job," I countered. "I'm a student now. And then next I'll be an actor."

Her eyes widened. "Whoa," she said. "Okay." You could see her mind searching for the right thing to say. "Well then. I guess you're kind of . . . fucked."

Amid my classes in voice, movement, and improvisation, I'd learned the valuable lesson that taste is subjective, that you can't waste your time worrying what other people think. You can't dwell on whether your roommate might be on to something when she calls you "fucked" after having seen you take the stage, because she, you remind yourself, likes Shania Twain and baby Ts. She, ergo, knows nothing. See, once you start questioning whether or not to spend another $25,000 a year on kettledrum bangers— if, per your mother's suggestion, you start wondering where all this acting training gets you *really*—your instructors instruct you away from the introspection necessary to realize you're wasting your time, money, and dignity. "Grow a thick skin," they say, "or you won't stand a chance in this business."

What they conveniently omit is that said "thick skin" is too often synonymous with a thick head. "Be stupid," they should say, "and possess not a lick of self-awareness. Otherwise, you won't stand a chance in this business."

A more honest assessment, it's one that described me precisely. Unconstructive criticism could only make me feel down. But not out. Never out. I'd raise my chin a little higher, tighten the laces on my jazz shoes just a little tighter. I'd throw my shoulders back and conceive of my next Afrocentric performance piece. I would soldier blindly forth.

6

albino

Every day I'd get a one-hour break from acting school, and while my more urbane classmates spent the hour lunching on grapes and goat cheese at a nearby Soho coffeehouse, I'd make the trek back to my dorm cafeteria for inexpensive cheesesteaks. These were solitary hours spent plotting my next student showcase or imagining sociopathic icebreakers I'd use to seduce Elijah:

1. *"'Sup, sexy?"*

   No, I thought, *wrong.*

   The "'sup" was too Brian Epstein, the "sexy" too forward. I'd be laying out my cards too quickly. There would be nothing left with which to backpedal if backpedal I must.

2. *"'Sup, my Negro?"*

   Vaguely racist. Wrong again.

3. *"Hi. Would you like to lay your chocolate skin beside my white . . . vagina?"*

Bingo.

Forward? Yes, but at least in a way that was over-the-top enough to suggest a decent sense of humor. A nip here, a tuck there, and the pickup line could work.

If the timing's right, I thought, *I'll roll with it.*

A fixture in the cafeteria as constant as the cheesesteaks was a borderline albino. She had red hair instead of white and blue eyes instead of pink, but her skin was strikingly pale, and every afternoon I'd see her reading a medical dictionary that she'd placed beside her lunch tray. Two groups of people read medical dictionaries: premed students and hypochondriacs. You can tell who's who because med students look bored, hypochondriacs enthralled. It's a lesson I learned after bearing witness to my mother's hypochondria. In my adolescence, she'd spend weekends sucking down FiberCon tablets, all the while paging through her own medical dictionary looking equal parts scared and excited. The albino looked the same: She'd turn a page, thrust a hand to a body part (breast, mole, underarm), check for a symptom. Most days she wore protective headwear—a visor, baseball cap, or afghan quilt—and often she'd be sobbing. One afternoon toward the start of first semester, I sat down at the table directly beside her to plot my next Elijah conquest (spoken-word poetry!) and overheard the beginnings of an especially vigorous fit. As a boisterous hysteric myself, tears attract rather than repel me, so I reached into my knapsack for a Kleenex.

"Tissue?" I offered.

The albino dragged her head up off the damp pages of her dictionary. "Is it scented?" she asked. "Scented tissues give me migraines."

Never in my life have I used a scented tissue; my mother swears that they cause cancer. "Scented?" I repeated. "My *god,* no. Of *course* not."

My *god*, no. Of *course* not. Like she'd asked some absurd question; like she'd asked if they'd been spun from gold or naval lint.

"Okay, then," she said, taking the tissue. "Thank you."

"No problem," I answered. "You can have the whole pack if you want."

I must admit my offer wasn't wholly altruistic; I had ulterior motives. You see, the albino, while paging through her medical dictionary, would simultaneously listen to a Walkman and sing aloud to herself, and she did so with surprising range and nuanced vibrato. Over the course of a month spent privy to her lunchtime vocal stylings, I began to imagine that she and I, a modern-day Roxie Hart and Velma Kelly, respectively, could form a traveling vaudeville-style act to earn an extra buck. Something called "Look Out, Boys!" or "Sara Barron Takes Manhattan!" The albino would sing while I joined in two-part harmony. Or played the recorder. Or recited Shakespearean monologues. All I'd been waiting for was the right moment in which to introduce myself. "Hey there!" I'd say. "I couldn't help but notice your beautifully nuanced vibrato. Perhaps later this week we could meet in the student activity center to practice two-part harmonies? What do you think of the title 'Sara Barron in the Big Bad Apple!'? And what're your thoughts on a 1920s theme? For costumes, of course; our oeuvre in terms of material would cover so much more. How much *Rent* do you know? How much Indigo Girls?"

On the day I offered up my tissue pack, however, the albino's mood seemed too unstable to be pitching performance ideas, and so instead, I just asked her what was wrong.

"I'm afraid of this mole," she said, and pointed to a minuscule spot on her forearm. "I was just sitting here eating my lunch, when all of a sudden I looked over at my arm and there it was. And for the life of me, I couldn't figure out if I'd ever seen it before. And then I thought, *No. Definitely not.* And *then* I thought, *Okay. So this is it: the beginning of the end. I'm on the cancer train toward melanoma.*"

Experience with my mother has taught me the dos and don'ts of handling a hypochondriac. You DON'T say, "That *is* weird," or, "Yikes!" or, "Whoa!" in response to anything short of a baseball-sized tumor. You DO treat them like they're crazy, shaking your head as you say, "You're crazy. There's no WAY that's melanoma!"

I looked at the albino's mole. I said, "You're crazy. There's no WAY that's melanoma."

"I hope you're right," she said, and took a deep breath, seemingly grateful for my sensitive words. "I don't want to die, you know?"

"I know," I said. "That would be . . . bad."

"And it'd be ironic too seeing as how I just started work on this performance piece called 'Death and Dying.'"

I sensed the content of the piece was supposed to be self-evident, but I cared to keep the conversation going.

"What's that about?" I asked.

"Death," she said. "And dying."

"Oh." I nodded. "Right. Well, that makes sense."

"I built this Grim Reaper out of papier-mâché and I waltz with him onstage while reciting my will over the first track off the Indigo Girls' *Rites of Passage* album."

The beginning of this conversation felt a lot like looking in a mirror. Like looking in a mirror, except for the fact that I'm not albino nor adept with papier-mâché, and neither am I terrified of death. I'm partial to hysterics at the prospect of dying *alone,* and, of course, paperwork, but the "It Must Be Cancer" shtick I've always left to my mother. This endeared me to her. It wasn't every day I met someone making theater pieces underscored by the Indigo Girls who appeared to be less emotionally stable than myself. And I'm of the mind-set that frequent hysterics are the geniuses among us, those wisely keyed in to the pointlessness and misery the more deluded can ignore. That, or they're self-indulgent to the point of incompetence. Regardless, I was lonely. And she seemed lonely, too. I thought of saying, "If you've got any free time over the course of the next sixty years, I'd like to grow old with you platonically," but

75

I didn't want to scare her. She'd endured enough for one day after having found a mole.

The albino's name was Maggie, and while I eventually succeeded in forcing her to be my friend, it took a good year's worth of effort. We'd both been placed in an Afro-Haitian dance elective our sophomore year at college, and with only three other people in the class, she had no choice but to talk to me. She was an acting major, too, she explained, "but one with an emphasis in experimental theater."

"But what do you experiment *with*?" I asked. To me, the pinnacle of theatrical expression lay in the movie version of *A Chorus Line*. I didn't understand the point of experimentation when such perfection had already been achieved.

"Anything," she answered. "Style. Form. Content . . . whatever." If I remember right, she used the phrase "to push the envelope" when describing her creative ambitions. I thought this sounded wonderfully rebellious and asked what else she'd done since "Death and Dying."

"A piece called 'Wiener Aktionismus,'" she answered, "based on the work of Hermann Nitsch and the rest of the Viennese Actionists."

If someone tries to talk theater with me but moves beyond the realm of musicals or Shakespeare's greatest hits, I'm lost. I told Maggie I had no idea what she was talking about, and she explained the Actionists as a group of Austrian performance artists who would wear all white, drench themselves in blood, skin animals, or urinate. "Wiener Aktionismus" was her homage. "Basically, I cover myself in fake blood that I've made from ketchup, then open a duffel bag, which is me pretending to birth myself from the belly of a cow, then I tear apart the duffel bag with a Swiss Army knife to signify the slaughter of the cow."

These sorts of antics perfectly illustrated the distinctions between Maggie and myself. While we both loved performing, I took to the stage for attention and approval. Maggie's goal, conversely, was audience alienation. She called it "Brechtian." I called it "embarrassing." I got dragged along whenever she needed assistance in what she called her "Happenings." Also inspired by the Actionists, these were performances in which Maggie staged public screaming matches. We'd go to a supermarket, for example, and pretend to be strangers fighting over a jar of peanut butter or a piece of produce. We'd start off quietly enough—"*I* was just about to take that cantaloupe"—then escalate the conversation until we were screaming loud enough and long enough to be escorted outside by the supermarket management. I always figured these shenanigans were Maggie's commentary on the self-absorbed, entitled nature of the human race, but recently I mentioned it and she explained otherwise. We'd gone for brunch at a diner around the corner from our old college dorm and the circumstances had me feeling nostalgic. "Remember sophomore year?" I asked. "When you were into that whole 'Happening' routine, and you'd drag me to the supermarket to stage those crazy fights? What was *that* about?"

"Nothing much." She shrugged. "I was just trying to be funny."

Maggie conceived of a half-dozen other performances addressing topics as diverse as her fear of Mickey Mouse masks, her oral-hygiene routine, and a bit called "Half-Assed" in which she'd cover her face with damp popcorn as a commentary on the pretentious nature of her acting instructors; I thought *those* were funny. But the "Happenings"? These were hours of my life spent shaming myself for her artistic vision! Perhaps I should've gotten angry, but the fact of the matter was that Maggie always returned the favor. I imagine she found my performances equally absurd, but still she'd do anything to help. She built me a papier-mâché microphone to use at home while practicing my spoken-word poetry. Also, there was a Barnes & Noble near our dorm that held a monthly open mic, and on those evenings we'd duet a variety of Indigo Girls songs. I'd force us to wear bandannas paired with flannel button-downs, and we were always surprised that none of the male participants ever asked us on a date. There was this one homeless man who came to all the shows, and one time he told Maggie she looked like "a white little alien; see-through, like!" but that's hardly a compliment. Really, it's insulting, and all it did was hurt her feelings. "Don't listen to him," I told her. "He's just some crazy homeless guy."

"But crazy homeless guys are honest," Maggie pointed out. "I bet I *do* look like an alien."

"You can't be serious!" I countered. "We're talking about a man who wears a diaper as a hat. These types cannot be trusted."

We established this sort of emotional support system and spent all our time together. My favorite thing about Maggie was that she, like a dog, was fiercely loyal. I gave her tissues when she cried, said her moles looked benign, embarrassed myself for her performance art, and for this she'd lash out violently at anyone who wronged me. If the phrase "she had my back" didn't evoke a pathetic attempt at urban authenticity, one to which I can't lay claim, then that's what I'd say about her. Instead, I'll stick to my dog comparison. New York, like the rest of the world, can be a horribly lonely place, and this makes loyalty an important aspect to a person. My parents had always provided me with a sense of security, but their approach was more restrained. When Brian Epstein made fun of my FUPA, for example, or when Randall Buckwald dumped me for that loosey-goosey lady colossus, my mother would jump to my defense and offer up supportive *words* ("What an asshole!" "He'll get his in the end!"), but Maggie, conversely, was the type to take *action*. One evening toward the end of our sophomore year, we rounded up two fake IDs, ventured to a downtown bar, and there was Maude, my freshman roommate. We hadn't seen each other in almost a year, and things had ended badly: Peggy Pearson, irate at having stepped in one of Maude's used sanitary pads, retaliated by emptying a can of tuna fish into her suitcase while we were all packing up. This revenge was exacted while Maude was out buying garbage bags and afterward, Peg dashed for the door without saying good-bye. Once Maude returned, she refused to believe Peg would do such a thing, and chose to blame me instead. Now here we were a year later, ten feet from each other, and she kept looking at me funny. En route to the bathroom, we overheard her say, "Sara . . . Barron . . . tuna . . . asshole . . ." I just shook my head, annoyed, but Maggie swung violently around as though she'd been socked in the jaw.

"WHAT?!" she screamed. Another noteworthy aspect to Maggie is that she has a low and powerful speaking voice. When she's mad, she bellows like she's giving birth. "DID YOU JUST CALL HER 'ASSHOLE'?" Maude looked terrified, like people do in horror movies when they realize their backwoods camping trip just took a nasty turn. "WELL, PEOPLE IN GLASS HOUSES SHOULDN'T THROW STONES, MAUDE! AND GIRLS WHO SPEND THEIR DAYS IN POOLS OF THEIR OWN URINE SHOUDN'T EVER REFERENCE TUNA! YOU STINK! I CAN SMELL YOUR PUSS FROM ALL THE WAY ACROSS THE BAR. IT'S TIME YOU CHANGED YOUR PAD!"

When college graduation rolled around, I was excited to introduce Maggie to my parents. To my mother specifically—I knew they'd bond over their shared fear of disease—and so I asked if I could bring her out to dinner.

"That's fine," said my mom, "but then please choose someplace cheap."

Later that night, my parents, brother, grandma, Maggie, and I all gathered at a spot called Dallas BBQ, a restaurant chain known for serving brick-sized slabs of meat for under twelve dollars. I ordered "The Wild West Combo," a tub of steak and shrimp.

"I don't think you need all that," said my grandmother. "You're already looking bloated."

"Oh, Mom," said my mom, "let her eat in peace. Bloated's not the worst thing. It's not cancer, at least."

Cancer mention. Cue Maggie.

"AMEN!" she shouted. Then she aggressively plunged her fork into a mound of iceberg lettuce while staring down my grandma. "And at least bloated goes away. Unlike wrinkles. They make a person look like a crumpled paper bag. *Forever.*"

My grandma's eyes narrowed. "There are creams," she seethed. "Creams can help."

"Not really," Maggie answered. Then she turned her attention to my dad. "Hey, Mr. Barron, can you please pass the bread?"

My father blushed, both at the formality of "Mr. Barron" and, more specifically, the adrenaline rush of seeing my grandmother taken to task. He passed the bread to Maggie. "Are you sure you wouldn't like something more to eat, dear?" he asked. "An order of fries? Creamed corn, perhaps?"

Maggie, a staunch vegetarian in a sea of beef and pork, had ordered only a small salad. "Oh no, I'm fine," she said. "I figured I ought to keep the tab down for the Jews, right? Ha-ha!"

Maggie's last name is McBrien and her nose is the size of a gum-drop. Add to that her albino-white visage and when she makes a Jew joke, you half expect a band of Nazi youth to march in behind her. As it happens, though, Maggie spent her late teens and early twenties immersed not only in the study of Judaic practices, but also in an obsessive preoccupation with conversion (she wrote a performance piece in 1999 entitled "My Shofar Is Sounding"). Maggie's got a near-rabbinic love of Judaism and, as such, immunity from accusations of anti-Semitism once you get to know her. As for my mother, it takes more than an Aryan-looking youth making reference to cheap Jews to unnerve her. My mother is not only aware of her frugality but prideful of it. Call her "cheap Jew" and she'll tell you "damn straight." Maggie made a lighthearted joke to validate her greatest source of pride, and she hopped giddily onboard.

"Ha-ha!" she laughed. "Oh, Maggie, you're funny. Any friend of my daughter's who orders on the cheap is a friend of mine, too!"

"I appreciate that," said Maggie. "As the Jews say, *l'chaim*!" She raised her glass for a toast. "Here's to health and new friends!"

In recent years, Maggie's mood has settled slightly thanks to a heavy, daily dose of Paxil, one she takes to mitigate the anxieties brought on by her hypochondria. So now she's less afraid of cancer, which is good, but somehow, impossibly, she's even more direct. It's like the Paxil pulverized whatever sliver of concern she possessed surrounding social graces and in so doing fostered an even bolder brand of directness that's all at once admirable *and* disconcerting. Just recently, Maggie went bicycle shopping with me. We bike shopped in Brooklyn, an intimidating task that involves the impatient condescension of men in stovepipe jeans. Well, not surprisingly, we were forced to endure a hip-strocity of a salesman who gave monosyllabic, seemingly tormented answers to every question I asked. Honestly, from the way this guy was acting, you'd have thought I was his mother berating him about his idiotic jeans. Maggie had had enough by minute ten.

"Excuse me, sir," she said, interrupting the eye-roll he'd offered in response to my question about warranties. "You're being very rude."

Hip-strocity was unconcerned. "Um"—he rolled his eyes again— "okay."

"No," she said, "it's not. And if you want my opinion, the problem is your jeans. They're so tight! I can see the nooks and crannies of your package, for god's sake. You can't possibly be comfortable. I say, head to the boys' room, give the sucker some air, then see if you feel like less of an asshole." Then she turned to me. "In the meantime, we're going somewhere where our business is appreciated."

While I value this sort of bravado, really it's the little things that keep us tied together through the years. It's the shared affection for the theater, the shared laughter at those less fortunate. "I might look albino," Maggie said after our run-in with Maude, "but at least I don't stink of rotten fish." It's the sense of protection she's afforded by my sensitivity to hypochondria and that I receive as the by-product of her oft-deranged forthrightness. And on the nights that my most pressing fear—not of death but of dying alone—looms large, it's the call that Maggie makes to say, "No. I won't allow that."

Coming from someone as crazily candid as she, I have no choice but to buy it.

the prophet needs
the boys' room

At the turn of the millennium, while others worried about Y2K and the possible end of the world, I obsessed over more important matters: Maggie had dared me to ask Elijah on a date. I told her my front-runner of a come-on line.

"Ingenious," she said. "'Would you like to lay your chocolate skin beside my white vagina?' Honestly, I'm jealous that I didn't think of that myself."

"It's funny *and* sexy!"

"A deadly combination."

We exchanged these words in public and to anyone who overheard us, we must have sounded strange, like Eastern European prostitutes who'd only just learned English.

A holiday soiree was coming up at my acting school and I thought it the perfect opportunity for a casual but flirtatious conversation between Elijah and me. There'd be free drinks and dancing and I planned to wear this slinky, red acrylic number. I also planned for Elijah to be drunk enough to think, *Sara Barron sure looks good in that slinky, red acrylic number*. Maggie agreed to accompany me there so as to act as personal cheerleader. "Go! Go! Go!" she'd shout whenever she saw Elijah disengaged from other conversations. I procrastinated for hours, however, until her enthusiasm waned. "You promised yourself you would," she reminded me. "I didn't come here to watch you dance alone to Matchbox 20 songs."

"I will," I said. "I swear I will. It's just, I'm waiting for the perfect time."

Maggie sighed and resigned herself to slumping in a corner while she checked for swollen glands. Once she found one, she went home.

"I'm leaving," she said. "I think I'm getting sick."

I let her go without protest, having established this sort of seductive solo jig to occupy myself: sidestep to the music, elbows pinned at my waist. Occasionally, I'd snap. I kept at this routine for the better part of an hour until I saw Elijah stumble drunkenly toward the door.

"ELIJAH!" I screamed; like both my parents, I've never been cool under pressure. I opt instead for screaming while sweating. "WAIT UP!" I screamed. "HOLD ON! DON'T GO! ELIJAH!"

My tall drink of water turned to see what all the fuss was about. "Oh hey," he said. "What's up?"

Suddenly, a mention of chocolate skin and/or white vaginas seemed a tad forward. I racked my brain for something more normal. I kept sweating.

"WHY ARE YOU LEAVING SO SOON?!" I asked.

"Because I'm drunk," he answered.

Over the course of my college career, I'd heard this rumor that drunk people were often willing to have sex more readily than sober people, and so I asked Elijah if he wouldn't like my company en route to his dorm. "I could walk you back," I offered. "If, you know, you'd like the company."

"Okay," he said, "I guess."

SARA BARRON

I have two favorite sex scenes in American cinema. The first occurs between Julia Roberts and Richard Gere in the delightful '90s smash *Pretty Woman*. Two thirds of the way through the film, there's this scene wherein Julia realizes she's developed feelings for her Dapper Dan, and then the two start humping feverishly atop high-thread-count sheets at the Beverly Wilshire Hotel. I also enjoy *The Sound of Music*, wherein the eldest of the Von Trapp children, Lisle, and her Nazi lover, Rolf, kiss in her father's garden gazebo. I've never been much of a Nazi supporter, personally, but I do *love* gazebos. They're so romantic! And what I imagined for Elijah and myself was a seamless blend of both impassioned scenes. We'd share a desirous outdoor kiss (albeit in the urban jungle in lieu of my father's Austrian estate), then make a dash for Elijah's dorm room for a lengthy bout of lovemaking over the course of which I'd be told repeatedly how both attractive and agile I was. I envisioned a lot of tender face-holding.

Instead, Elijah only asked if I would pee on him.

It happened rather quickly. We got to his dorm, he thrust me toward the bathroom, laid his gorgeous frame across the bathtub floor, and shouted, "PEE ON ME!"

I took a pause. I mean, I knew I *could* pee—I'd downed a jug of lobster bisque for dinner—but did that mean I *should* pee? Was this what people did? Did Peggy? Did Maggie? If so, what happens once you're done? Do you wipe? Who cleans up? There were these questions and a myriad of others. Namely, when asked to pee on a person, shouldn't you make absolutely sure you've heard correctly? Shouldn't you respond by asking, "You'd like for me to pee on you? Is that correct?" Perhaps this is a fussy way to go about it, but I think the interruption to the mood is worth it lest you let loose in a manner unsolicited.

For example, Elijah lay prostrate in his tub and shouted, "PEE ON ME!"

So I repeated, "Pee on you? You'd like for *me* to pee on *you*, is that correct?"

"Go, girl!" he shouted back. I thought this phrase had been

84

reserved for tired sitcom scripts, but apparently no. It had not. "Do your thing!" he squealed. "Pee on me!"

To be clear: this wasn't *my* thing. It was his. But I was twenty, spineless, and adoring, so in the end I followed through. I crouched awkwardly atop this strange and swarthy Denzel demigod and, presented with the options of To Pee or Not to Pee, decided: pee. I let my crushing need to please kick in before my dignity. Though in the moment it happened, it felt less like some dramatic abandonment of self than perhaps I've just described. Sex and urination had been closely intertwined in my formative years after all, so I guess I wrote it off as nothing too bizarre. I wrote it off, we toweled, and then we went to bed.

As far as I'm concerned, once you pee on a person, you two are boyfriend/girlfriend. You've made A Connection; you've shared Something Special. Hence my shock at Elijah's elusive attitude the following morning. I'd planned a packed itinerary of intercourse, then spooning, then a romantic pancake breakfast, but Elijah had other plans: first, to vomit the alcohol out of his system, then to excuse himself to a dormitory breakfast of his own. Whether or not he had pancakes I don't know as I wasn't asked to join him. He'd said, "Um. Okay. Well. Bye," then opened his front door to let me know to leave. I caught a faint hint of vomit on his breath intermingled with a fainter hint of Listerine.

I hesitated. I asked, "Huh?" I was confused and unprepared to go. I couldn't believe two people could share something as intimate as peeing and then not spoon. I couldn't believe I'd made it to the Promised Land and now would leave with nothing to show for it save an empty bladder.

Elijah repeated, "Um. So. Yeah. I'll see you. I guess. So. Yeah. Bye."

I managed a half wave and slinked out the door feeling rejected and alone, those all-too-frequent by-products of being twenty and adoring.

Later that afternoon, Maggie called to ask me how it went. "Did you get jungle fever?" she asked. "Did Elijah?"

That phrase, beyond its usual connotation of interracial attraction, evokes something primal. It's the word *jungle* that does it.
And if there's one act more primal than sex, it's got to be a hearty
pee.

"As a matter of fact, yes," I answered. "Elijah got it bad."

For a day, I let Maggie think that meant that I got laid instead
of asked to pee. But ours was not a friendship built of lies. We met
up later that same night for dorm food and a movie, and after
greeting me with a tailor-made singsong salutation ("HE'S GOT
JUNGLE FEVER, *SHE'S* GOT JUNGLE FEVER!"), after an
hour spent pressed for every nitty-gritty detail, I finally came
clean.

"Look," I admitted, "I didn't have sex with Elijah."

Maggie's face fell. "But I said, 'jungle fever,' and you—"

"I know. But what I meant was that I peed."

"You peed?"

"Yes. I peed. On him. Yes."

"On purpose?" she asked. "You peed *on* him *on* purpose?"

"He asked me to."

"And you said yes?"

"I thought it was foreplay. Pee now, sex later. But it didn't work
that way: I peed, we slept, he puked. The end."

"No make-out?"

"No."

"No sex?" she probed. "No spooning?"

"No and no," I answered. "Nothing. This morning he shuffled
me out the door in less time than it had taken me to pee the night
before. It was so degrading. He made me feel so embarrassed."

Someone other than Maggie might, in that moment, have
placed a comforting hand on my shoulder, acknowledged Elijah's
insensitivity, then nudged me gently toward a lesson learned:
Don't have sex with someone who responds to your advances by
saying "I guess." Don't have sex with someone who's about to
vomit. Don't pee if you don't really want to pee. I mean, sure,
Elijah's behavior had been less than upstanding, but I'd made

missteps, too. I'd gotten myself into this pissing pickle on my own. I'd ignored blatant signs and indulged silly expectations. And someone other than Maggie might have objectively considered all this. But objective wasn't Maggie's style.

"If *he* embarrassed *you*," she growled, "then it's our turn to return the favor."

Maggie, Elijah, and I all took a history of theater class together Monday mornings. It was held in a two-hundred-seat lecture hall, and Maggie and I always sat toward the back scribbling textbook notations and catnapping, respectively. Maggie's the studious type and I've been blessed with the ability to reach the REM stage while resting my chin against my sternum. Anyway, the Monday class following the interracial urinary debacle, Maggie greeted Elijah with a special salutation of his own. The second he walked through the door, she screamed his name so loud, I *swear* I saw the teacher's glass shake atop his podium.

"ELIIIIIIIIIJAAAAAAAAAAH!" she howled.

All hundred-plus students turned to look at her. Then him. She stayed relaxed in her chair, her feet propped comfortably atop the seat in front of her, while Elijah stared back dumbstruck. **"WHAT'S UP WITH THE PEEING?"**

"What peeing?" asked a classmate. Maggie relished the encouragement.

"OH, I'LL TELL YOU WHAT PEEING," she answered. **"THAT GUY BROUGHT MY FRIEND HERE"**—and she pointed to me—**"UP TO HIS DORM ROOM LAST FRIDAY NIGHT, THEN HOPPED IN HIS BATHTUB AND TOLD HER TO PEE ON HIS CHEST."** The class turned collectively from Maggie to Elijah, anxious for his explanation. **"AND TO EACH HIS OWN IF THAT'S WHAT YOU'RE INTO. BUT THEN AFTERWARD HE HAD THE NERVE TO TOSS HER OUT LIKE DAY-OLD GARBAGE! WHAT GIVES, FREAK?! WHAT GIVES?!"**

Elijah turned purple like an eggplant but was saved from having to answer for himself by the teacher's arrival; Maggie, the stalwart confronter, was nevertheless a diligent student who wished to stay in her professor's good graces, so she shut her mouth once he walked through the door. This was fine by Maggie—she'd said her piece—and fine by me, too. I'd felt justified just by watching her performance. And perhaps this was absurd. Perhaps I, as the peeer, should have been embarrassed, too. But I was too busy enjoying myself, too busy basking in the glory of having watched Elijah squirm. It felt so comforting, so wonderful. Better, if you can possibly imagine, than a whole morning's worth of spooning ever could.

8

a little bit of mania

New York City is a dirty place. Giuliani's mayoral tenure may have helped the smut side of the problem, but it did nothing for pollution. The air here is thick with exhaust, and when I wash my face at the end of a day, a sheet of filth flushes into the sink. It's an aspect of city living that's proven tough on my skin. Two months after I moved here, my entire body exploded in a batch of acne so severe my pimples looked like kernels of corn on a cob. On my face mostly, but my legs, chest, back, and buttocks were also afflicted. The leg stuff was what really threw me for a loop. I didn't know that acne on an ankle was something that could happen to a person, but that fall I learned, yes. As with so many things, if the timing's right and the stars align, anything *is* possible. This adage usually evokes an inspirationally poignant or dramatic scene—a homeless man turned lawyer, a boy band of Iraqi refugees—but for me, it only meant I'd found a whitehead on my thigh.

Like a missing eye or disabling limp, acne is a problem to which the outside world is privy. This is what makes it so hard to endure.

I'm not saying I would've preferred something more externally discreet, like leukemia or a brain tumor, but there was something about the acne, specifically, that encouraged people to talk to me about it. It was as if, because the problem seemed more solvable than, say, the aforementioned missing eye, random strangers thought it was appropriate to offer up advice. At a Starbucks or the post office—any public spot would do—I fielded regular interruptions to my day. "Hey there" or "Excuse me" served as the conversational entrée, followed by a "I couldn't help but notice that . . . ," or "I don't mean to be rude, but . . ." Then they'd describe *my* acne *to* me and tell me what they thought I ought to do to fix it.

"Excuse me, I don't mean to be rude—gosh, I hope this isn't completely out of line—but I just wanted to say that I spotted you across the room." I'd dreamed of having these words said to me, just never in reference to my acne. "And, well, I noticed what was going on with your skin." Here he'd motion with his hand to signal the specific region being referenced: chin, hairline, or sternum. "And I just wanted to tell you that I had exactly the same problem up until a year ago. And the only thing that worked for me was" fill in the blank. Some said Accutane, others mentioned Proactiv, some professed a stalwart allegiance to the birth control pill or a heavy diet of red and yellow vegetables. "Anyway, I only said something because I was hoping to be helpful. So. Well. I hope I was. Have a great day!" I liked to imagine the version of our interaction he'd later relay to a spouse or coworker, one that painted him as dermatologic hero, someone selfless enough to run the risk of my potential wrath for the chance to help me turn my face around. "I thought, *I have to do this,*" he'd say. "I have the chance to help her!" I didn't mind doing these people the favor of this boost to their self-confidence, but as for what it did to mine? Nada. I'd tried and failed with all their suggestions before. Confronted with the internal organ–melting powers of something like Accutane, my acne scoffed, "HA!" Because my problem wasn't hormones. My problem wasn't skin care.

My problem was my trichotillomania.

Since birth, I've indulged this crushing impulse to pick at every corner of my person. I live with clawed-out cuticles and calluses, I pluck out arm hair strand for strand, I clip at fleshy skin tabs with a nail clipper. I also enjoy scratching the underside of my right elbow (the left does nothing for me) until the skin turns candy-apple red. I don't know why I carry out these layman's mutilations; I only know it feels right. It's a sort of behavior classified as trichotillomania, and I was diagnosed at ten after my mother found me crouched on the back porch, gnawing at my callused foot.

"WHAT ARE YOU DOING?!" she howled when she saw me. It was a fair enough question, but she'd interrupted my meditative state and I was unprepared to answer. I'd never given any thought to what I was doing and why. It was just a thing I did. Like if you're thirsty, drink water. If your bladder's full, pee. If you're bored, stick your heel in your mouth. It was the course of action that felt natural.

"What?" I asked back hazily. Chewed callus flaked my lips. "What did you say?"

To hear my mother's version of these same events, I looked dead in the eyes, and the image was so disturbing she convinced herself I'd been infected by a rabid dog. With a few calm words and the assistance of the medical dictionary, my father managed to ease her toward the realization that *acting* like a rabid dog didn't mean I'd been *infected* by a rabid dog, and that perhaps, rather than an ER visit, a smarter course of action would be an appointment with a therapist. So one week later I went to see her colleague, Dr. Barbra Levy, who sat me on her couch, handed me a stress-reliever ball, and fired off a half dozen questions: "Do you find yourself pulling your hair? Picking your skin? Do you know why you do it? Do you know why it feels good? Do you do it at a certain time of day? What would happen if you felt the urge to pick and didn't follow through?"

This last question struck me as absurd. To me, it sounded like, "What if you felt the urge to *breathe* and didn't follow through?"

Well, then I'd die, obviously, and death was not an option. I was battling trichotillomania, for god's sake, not a suicidal outlook.

I told Dr. Levy that her question confused me. "I *have* to follow through," I said.

"No," she corrected, "you *want* to. You don't *have* to. Try to think about the difference."

The attempt at self-empowerment was nice but nevertheless naive and deeply idiotic. I mean, you could mince words with a crackhead, for example, but a lot of good that'll do. Get yourself a rock of crack and ask the aforementioned addict to babysit it for a while. Tell her, "You just *like* crack. You don't *need* it! See you in an hour!" and I'll bet my uterus and every chance at future happiness that crack rock's gone once you get home. Similarly, I may have just *wanted* to uproot an ingrown hair, but a lot of good that distinction did me if withholding prompted a panicked descent into oblivion, this imagined universe in which I was slathered in calluses and foot-long fleshy skin tabs, a fit of nightmarish afflictions I'd be forbidden to remove.

Dr. Levy diagnosed my trichotillomania, and the lengths she went to solve it involved instructing me to sing or whistle instead of indulging my more natural instincts.

"What if you—hmm, let's see—your mommy told me you like singing. What's your favorite song?"

Now here, finally, was an easy question. "'Rum Tum Tugger,'" I answered, "from *Cats*."

"All right. So what if you sang 'Rum Tum Tugger' every time you felt like pulling at your arm hair? Or what if you whistled! What if you whistled, instead, a song that made you feel really happy?!"

And what if, by chance, a massive, caged pig were to suddenly take flight? I could no sooner tra-la-la my way through "Rum Tum Tugger" as a substitute for hair pulling than I could force my own spontaneous combustion. Dr. Levy's suggestions were impossible, and as a result, my trichotillomania ran rampant. Over time, my parents learned to cope with my disorder. In 1996, I discovered that chewing pen caps was a helpful substitute for chewing on my nail beds, so that year my mom bought me a bar-relful of Bic pens at Costco for Hanukkah. This course of action was something Dr. Levy might have called "enabling," but that was fine by my mom seeing as how she wasn't dealing with a fatal illness. "I mean, sure it's strange," she'd tell her friends. They'd come over for coffee and spot me sprawled on the living room couch, maniacally scratching my right arm. "But the way *I* think of it is, at least it's not cancer, you know? I mean, I'd rather have her clawing out her arm hair than smoking cigarettes."

The side effects of my trichotillomania (thinned-out hair, rav-aged feet, and so on) weren't ideal, but they were tolerable if it meant not having to give up my vice. But my move to New York changed all that. My skin's adjustment to the aforementioned residue of über-urban living facilitated, at first, a faint smattering of blemishes. I was someone who'd complain about *a* zit. I'd spot one and then, regardless of time or location, be forced by my trichotillomania to immediately remove it. Whether riding on the subway or staring in a bathroom mirror, whether readied, lush whitehead or deep-rooted welt, I'd attack, remove, and wake the next morning to find two where one had been the night before. By the end of month one, this rule of multiples made it clear I had a problem; by the end of month two, I looked positively diseased. I couldn't wear my glasses anymore because the inches of skin from eye to hairline were splattered by acne that ran deep and wide, and the pressure from the stems against them was too painful to endure. When my parents saw me at Thanksgiving for the first time since leaving for college, my father cried. Initially, he tried to play it off like it was just that he was happy to see me, but tears of joy aren't usually underscored by the phrase "Oh god, what happened?" My days were spent multitasking, going about my acting classes or spoken-word performances, all the while parading my hands along my face like a blind girl reading Braille. I'd be in search of a newly clogged pore, a painful monstrosity I loathed but—strangely—still loved, as I considered it a plaything.

After one solid year spent slathered in layers of fresh boils and

old scars, Maggie decided it was time to intervene. She wasn't
worried about the cosmetic ramifications, but she *was* sure I was
dying. We'd pass the time together listening to CDs or writing creative theater pieces, and frequently she'd turn around to find me
driving my fingers toward the root of some most recent find along
my hairline.

"STOP!" she'd scream. "YOU HAVE TO STOP! YOU'RE
KILLING YOURSELF! YOU'RE GOING TO DIE!" Maggie's
fear was that instead of getting something toxic out, I was driving
something toxic in, toward my brain, at which point I was sure to
contract a fatal infection and die.

"I don't think it works that way," I said.

"Shows what you know," she snapped back. "I saw a show once
on the Discovery Health Channel and that's exactly what happened. This girl wouldn't stop picking at a zit that was right above
her ear, and eventually she drove the bacteria into her brain, and
for days she was nauseous and dizzy. Then she died."

Every addict who recovers has her turning point, a moment
wherein she is ready to "Make the Choice to Change." That's a
phrase of Dr. Levy's. I wasn't ready at twelve or sixteen, when
tweezing hair in lieu of shaving was more fun for me than my
Oral-B electric toothbrush. But by nineteen, I was ready. I guessed
Maggie's story regarding the lethal zit was fake, so it wasn't so
much the risk of death that tricked me into changing; it was the
eventual, surprising onset of boredom. Like finally, I'd had my
fill; like my trichotillomania had forced me into thinking of my
acne as an activity, and now I needed a vacation. When Maggie
relayed to me her cautionary tale, I guess I'd been in some more
willing place mentally. Not willing to believe a person dies from
popping pimples, but willing to believe that change was possible.
For weeks I kept up with my old habits, all the while considering
whether or not I could quit them if I had to. There'd be a black-
head blooming on my chin and I'd think, "Could you restrain
yourself? Let's say your father's life was on the line." I wouldn't
test myself, but I'd *think* about testing myself. I decided to share

this bit of progress with Maggie in the hope that she'd encourage me. She did.

"How wonderful!" she cried. "So now we've got to get you to actually stop instead of just thinking about it. We have to retrain your mind so that the face-clawing, the arm-scratching, all of it, becomes something you associate with bringing pain instead of pleasure." She thought about it for a moment, drumming her fingers on her knees. "How about this?" she exclaimed. "How about every time I see you touch your face, I punch you? Over time you'd learn to stop, don't you think? If it was the only way to get me to stop hitting you?"

Maggie may be tiny—she has baby hands; her palms are smaller than a pair of tangerines—but she nevertheless lacks the emotional stability a person ought to have to whom you give carte blanche to punch you. I asked for other options.

"What if I pinched you instead?" she suggested. "Or pulled your hair? Or kicked your shins?"

I wanted to say, "Well, that sounds dangerous and traumatic," but I knew if I did, Maggie would counter by telling me that was the point. So I went the alternate route of explaining that there was no way someone with hands as tiny as hers could ever seem threatening and that consequently, her attempts at personalized Pavlovian conditioning seemed doomed to fail. Maggie considered my point and said, "Okay, so then what if I screamed at you instead? What if every time I saw you touch your face I screamed, 'STOP! DON'T TOUCH YOUR FACE! STOP!' directly in your ear?"

Because Maggie's voice is so shockingly loud, it seemed plausible that this could work effectively as a deterrent. It seemed plausible I'd pay the price of my trichotillomania if it meant she'd be kept quiet.

"All right," I said, and bit the bullet of the panic kicking in. "Scream. Scream directly in my ear."

For the next three months, Maggie passed her time in fits of piercing hysteria. A dozen times a day she'd scream, "STOP! DON'T DO IT! STOP!" every time she saw me reaching for my battered face. An exhausting process for the both of us, it was complicated by the fact that one month in, Maggie's next-door neighbors complained to the dormitory RA, fearing Maggie was either a) schizophrenic, or b) fielding a violent attack. The knock on the door surprised us both.

"The girls next door said they heard a woman screaming," said the RA. "Is everything okay?"

Maggie assured her things were fine. "It's just, my friend here has this weird disease that makes her pick her face and pull her hair and tweeze her pubes, and I'm trying to get her to stop."

The pube's mention was gratuitous, I thought, and this left me feeling overly exposed and angry at Maggie. But also, I'd been cured. Well, *cured* is the wrong word. More precisely, I'd been pushed into recovery. Day by day, scream by scream, my brain had started to rewire itself. Not from wanting to indulge my trichotil-lomaniac's tendencies altogether, but now that my stronger impulse was to silence Maggie, they did become more manageable. And I stayed on track because my skin had finally started getting better. There was this square inch of my cheek that, having resembled a grotesquely textured honeycomb of acne for almost a year, now looked like human skin again! This simple feat thrilled me; it was just the stuff to keep me focused. After three months, I stopped with my obsessive actions and Maggie stopped her screaming. After six months, I looked normal. A worthwhile reward, no doubt, but that didn't mean that getting there was easy. It wasn't. It *isn't*. My skin still breaks out (every week of premenstruation, every holiday season when I eat grease and choco-late by the gallon). And through it all I must not touch my face lest the downward spiral start again. I continue to restrain myself. New pimples come and I withhold. "Not today," I say. "Just make it through today, then pop the Jesus out of it tomorrow." Time and again I've played this trick, and that's how I get through. Like an on-the-wagon alcoholic: one day at a time.

Friends and family applauded my success at beating my addic-tion. People were impressed because people love redemptive tales.

Snort crack, screw for money, remove your pubic hair with rusty tweezers, and still you'll be lauded. Just as long as you inch toward the goal of self-improvement; as long as you say later, "Now I know better." People love to forgive how troubled you were, just as long as you reform. You get so much more credit than if you'd been normal to begin with.

Nowadays I'm a waitress, and lately my mother's been suggesting I do something more with my life. "How much longer do you think this waiting tables thing will last?" she asks. "One year? Or two? Maybe three?"

This makes me wonder if perhaps I shouldn't take up some other compulsive addiction, just so I can conquer it and once again be perceived as accomplished.

"What's new with Sara?" one might ask.

"Well, Sara *finally* kicked her meth addiction. It was *so* very difficult. We're *so* very proud."

"Recovered Meth Addict" would look great on my otherwise unimpressive résumé while simultaneously placing my knack for garden-variety underachievement into clear perspective. My mom might not be impressed that I wait tables, but if I quit smoking crystal meth *and* wait tables? Now that would be impressive.

I hear meth is bad for your skin, though. Perhaps I ought to choose another vice.

9

non-equity

I studied acting for four years at the university level and received a BFA. That stands for Bachelor of Fine Arts to most, but my mother's favorite joke was that it stood instead for Big Fucking Actor. "Look who it is!" she'd say when I'd fly home to visit. "My big fucking actor of a daughter!" My stock response was "Very funny," to which she'd reply, "Well, I thought we ought to laugh instead of cry about it."

"It" was the hour of reckoning: I had my BFA, my memorized monologue. I'd re-soled my jazz shoes and purchased a beret. It was time to scrap the "student" portion from my title and graduate to "Actor."

Ever watch TV? See a movie? Attend a Broadway show? If so, perhaps you've noticed acting as a career path for the physically attractive. Some of the beauties can act to boot, but first and foremost they're oddly and unfairly pretty. On the attractiveness scale from one to ten, these girls are tens. Conversely, I was not. I'm not gratuitously self-deprecating. I'm just being realistic. Sporting a

FUPA and faint wisps of back hair, I hung just left of center: a four. Stilettos, a hint of rouge, a nicely tailored dress—these devices inch me toward a five, a six *at best*. But you wouldn't stop me on the street to say, "You ought to be in pictures!" And were you privy to one or another of my college acting projects—let's say you'd been at Barnes & Noble's magazine rack on the night I hit the open mic—then you, like Peggy Pearson, would have told me not to quit my day job. And you, like Peggy Pearson, would have been ignored. I clung to my acting ambitions like a million others so clearly destined to fail because the sparest shred of talent (I *do* do a great Tina Turner impersonation) mixed with a pinch of encouragement and the desperate hope for fame can convince you to pursue a ludicrous ambition. *I have to be an Actor!* you decide. *I can't live a Life of Regret!*

You're primed to try. And primed to fail.

One Sunday morning not long after my college graduation, I was on the phone with my mother. "Just called for a chat with my big fucking actor," she announced. "How's it going, anyway?"

People love to ask you how it's going when you're in hot pursuit of an acting career. Unstable artistic paths attract this line of questioning and it's ironic, I think, seeing as how the honest answer is almost always "bad." Variations include "very bad" or "soul-suckingly bad." Any actor who says otherwise is lost in a maze of denial and the reason is this: Actors with careers on the upswing don't get asked the question in the first place, since, in accordance with the nature of the beast, everyone already knows. Everyone's seen him/her in that movie starring Colin Farrell, the Tylenol commercial, the walk-on role in a *CSI* show. So instead of questions getting asked, praise is given: "You were wonderful in that Tylenol commercial!"

A successful actor needn't explain herself nor laundry list her accomplishments; she's too busy basking in her public praise. In contrast, it's the rest of us who must hone our desperate mantras. Asked how the acting's going, we throw down the card of overcompensation.

"How's the acting going?"

"Great!" we say. "*So* great!" Then we forgo specific details with a qualifying statement like, "I've got an audition," or "I landed a callback." So vast are the variations on what this could entail, they do nothing to support a claim of greatness. But it's all we have to cling to and therefore all we ever say.

I'd go exactly this route with my mother.

"So how's the acting going for my big fucking actor?"

"Great, Mom! Really great. I've got an audition on Tuesday for this one play called *Feelin' Fine,* then another one on Wednesday for an improv troupe, then another on Friday for a disco-danced version of *A Midsummer Night's Dream.*"

"Anything paid?"

"What?"

"Anything *paid*?"

This question confused me. Four months on the audition circuit, and a word like *paid* had lost its meaning. It seemed completely out of context when mentioned in regards to acting. It was as though I'd said, "I've got an audition!" and my mother had followed up by asking, "Chicken or beef?" It all felt very disconnected.

To support myself, I worked the evening shift at a Banana Republic in Soho, where I learned how to properly fold a button-down shirt. Then I'd spend my days auditioning feverishly. I was like a madwoman, having decided that what I lacked in cuteness, I'd make up for in drive. Another woman might have the fuller head of well-groomed hair, the more shapely, toned physique, but I'd work harder. I'd audition for *anything.* In one week, I tried out for the role of a street whore named Lavinia in a triple–Off Broadway production of Bernard Shaw's classic *Androcles and the Lion,* to which I wore my beret and engaged in the following dialogue with a raging homosexual who read the role of Army Captain:

> *"You are brave, Captain!"*
> *"Do you mock me, whore?"*

"*Not I, Captain!*"

"*Do you even know how true Christians love, you whore?*"

This was followed by an audition for a student film pitched as *Melrose Place* meets *Roots,* then an original play entitled *Take Me as I Am* about pedophilia as a disease to be understood rather than reviled, then Brecht's *Mother Courage and Her Children,* then the part of Woodland Nymph #4 in an avant-garde perform-ance piece called *Fly Like the Wind, Geronimo.* Maggie and I went to this last one together after Maggie saw it listed on a flyer in her local diner. The flyer said the producers wanted sixteen bars of an up-tempo song, so I chose the Merman standard "There's No Business Like Show Business," made it to bar num-ber ten, and was promptly asked to leave. I waited for Maggie out-side the audition studio nursing a juice box before she emerged, ectastic.

"I got a callback!" she shouted. "The director called me 'organ-ically magical'!"

"What's that supposed to mean?"

Maggie didn't know for sure but learned the rough translation at the callback.

"Will you go onstage naked," asked the director, "as you mime being stuck in a box?"

Maggie was deeply insulted, told him no, and stormed out the door. "How degrading is *that*?!" she asked me later.

"Very."

"I mean, public nudity's no walk in the park to begin with. But nothing's worse than"—a look of fear and disgust overtook her—"*mime.*"

The first callback I ever got was for a sketch comedy group called Lil' Devils. The group's creative director asked that I improvise a scene about Mary-Kate and Ashley Olsen having sex with each other, which, frankly, I nailed. (Pun intended!) I had the whole production team in stitches as I performed Mary-Kate atop her twin in reverse-cowgirl position, hammering away until she bruised her own pelvis and cracked her sister's ribs. Not only was I being funny, I thought, but I was also commenting on the negative side effects of anorexia in Hollywood! This sort of multilayered artistry was rewarded with a callback, yes, but not an actual part. For as gifted as I may have been at mimed celebrity incest, I'm not good at impressions. I mean, sure, my Tina Turner can stop traffic, but the folks at Lil' Devils needed someone with a solid Walken or DeNiro.

This tease and denial of the callback broke my father's heart. "Did you hear back about the sketch comedy group?" he'd ask expectantly. He wanted so badly to have something to show off about. At various weddings and Bat or Bar Mitzvahs, we'd both had occasion to endure the gloating parents of other commercial actors.

"Did you see Kimmy in the Herbal Essences commercial?! She's the girl whose hair gets frizzy from the rain?! Wasn't it *AMAZING*?" The way they carry on, you'd think their child won the Nobel Prize or, at the very least, contributed to society in some microscopic sliver of a way instead of mugging for the camera about freesia-scented styling gel. My father craved a taste of this same sort of undue pride.

"Dad, this is tough to tell you, but I think that Lil' Devils sketch group went with someone else."

"*What?*"

"I think they needed someone better at impressions."

"But did they *hear* you sing?! Did you *do* your Tina Turner?!"

He was more deluded than a porky pageant mother. He could not understand how anyone, having borne witness to my version of "Proud Mary," would—*could!*—deny me the chance of an awed, adoring crowd. I imagined my mother trying to explain it.

"Joe, it's time to accept that maybe acting isn't Sara's forte."

"*What?*" He'd try to convince himself that she was the one who'd gone mad. "Have you gone *mad*?!"

"No." She'd stay calm. "I have not. Now let's focus on the positives: She doesn't have cancer. She doesn't do drugs. She's learned to fold shirts at Banana Republic."

My mother had begun to make progress, combating the shared hopes and dreams of my father and me, when the impossible occurred and I scored a part. Two, actually. I'd be playing the dual roles of Orange Girl and Sister Marthe in a quintuple–Off Broadway production of *Cyrano de Bergerac*.

"Where's 'quintuple–Off Broadway'?" asked my mom. I could hear the air quotes in her voice. "Downtown? Uptown? Brooklyn? Queens?"

"New Jersey," I answered.

"Do they have theaters in New Jersey?"

They do, in fact, though this particular production would be mounted in the director's apartment, in the living room he'd partitioned off with shower curtains.

"New Jersey *has* theaters," I explained, "though I, personally, will be performing in a much more avant-garde space than that."

"Where?"

"A loft."

Loft sounded artier than *Jersey apartment*.

"Are you getting paid?"

"What?"

"Are you getting paid?"

"I'm not sure I understand the question."

As far as I was concerned, the opportunity to play the dual parts of Orange Girl and Sister Marthe was payment enough. Orange Girl (lest you've forgotten her noteworthy scene in act I) sells her goods to fellow villagers. She asks, "Oranges? Milk? Raspberry syrup? Lemonade?" And then just after Cyrano's entrance, after he's said, "One more word of that same song, and I destroy you all!" Orange Girl exclaims, "What an outrage!"

I'd say both those lines and then have two and a half hours to kill "backstage" before reemerging in act V as Sister Marthe. I'd say, "Sister Claire stole a plum out of the tarte this morning!"

just minutes before (spoiler alert!) Cyrano confesses his love for Roxane and dies.

I'd use my rehearsal time to practice alternate line readings ("WHAT an outrage. What an OUTRAGE!"), a diligence I hoped would impress the director, but it seemed rather to annoy him. One day I let one slip that was especially robust:

> Cyrano: *One more word of that same song, and I destroy you all!*
> Orange Girl: *WHAT AN OUTRAGE!!!*

The director got angry. "JESUS *CHRIST*!" he shouted from his living room couch. "Sara, I need—*NEED!*—for you to tone it down, okay?"

"Toning it down," I repeated, and did a little salute, "toning it down."

This was a trick I'd learned in acting school: When you, the actor, are given a direction, you repeat it back to prove your understanding, e.g.:

"Sara, move back. You're supposed to be *behind* Roxane."

"Moving back, sir, moving back."

"Can all the nuns exit stage right?"

"Exiting stage right, sir, exiting stage right!"

I considered this the height of professional behavior, yet for all my fellow cast mates it seemed to connote my possible battle with autism: Every time I did it, they'd give me wide-eyed and bewildered looks, the worst of which came from the actress playing Roxane. A doe-eyed eighteen-year-old who, when not busy giving me the are-you-autistic eye, indulged in this horrific habit of calling me "sweetie." I have a rule of thumb with that word: If I'm older and fatter than you, don't use it to address me.

"Hey, sweetie!" she'd say while practicing one of her big, dramatic scenes. "If you've got a sec, can you do me the biggest favor *ever*?" I always had "a sec"; I had three lines. "Can you run to the deli and get me a Coke?"

With nothing else to do and without the backbone needed to say no, I'd agree to her biddings. Then en route I'd count the reasons I despised her:

1. Roxane called me "sweetie."

2. Roxane had big, beautiful eyes.

3. Roxane called herself "a guy's girl." "I'm just a guy's girl!" she'd explain to Christian the heartthrob or Ragueneau the bread-shop owner. "Girls can be *so* catty, you know? So all my friends are always guys!" This common rumination disgusts me every time I hear it. Disguised as some pathetic attempt at an independent streak, what someone really ought to say is, "My ability for interpersonal connection begins and ends with my need for sexual approval!" This sort of woman flips her lid at the chance to bowl or check the football score and for such penchants she expects a fat helping of attention. Preferably male. For my part, I prefer the title Girl's Girl. Not contingent on a penchant for fruity alcoholic drinks (though I do *love* a double amaretto on the rocks), the foundation for my claim is this: Between me and *my* close friends, flirtation and sexual tension needn't be the building blocks.

4. Roxane was eighteen, and eighteen made me feel old. I may have been just five years older, but the thing about aspiring to act is that *anything* can make you feel old. You're over the hill by the time you're twenty-six. They don't tell you that in acting school, they don't say, "Ditch all this: Lose thirty pounds, audition *NOW!*" though such advice would prove more helpful than what they *do* dole out on chakras and vocal technique. It's true some successful starlets don't hit their stride until they're twenty-six, but hitting a stride by twenty-six means you've been booking commercials since you were ten. If by twenty-six you've worked little enough that there's still room on your résumé for a show you did in college, good luck. You'll need it. If someone has legally rented a car *and* uttered the phrase "I'm

thinking of giving acting a shot," she's in trouble—just as deluded, I believe, as my father and I.

Roxane, in all her resplendent teenage-ness, made me consider all these harsh realities. She'd set my wheel of unpleasant thought in motion every single day and forced me toward a revelation: This acting thing might not pan out. To be fair, it wasn't just Roxane that did it. It was Roxane *plus* the commute to New Jersey *plus* the "theater" in New Jersey *plus* the shower-curtain stage in the theater in New Jersey. There was also the issue of my costume, which in the role of Sister Marthe included a habit made of felt and paper towel. There are only so many times you can layer those fabrics on your head before you wonder what the fuck it is you're doing, only so many times you can practice lines like "Raspberry syrup? Lemonade?" before your mind begins to wander and the pressing questions get too pressing to ignore.

Is this all there is?

Is this a bad idea?

Is there a God?

Am I an asshole?

If I punch Roxane the next time she says "sweetie," how will she react?

With two months of rehearsal, I had a lot of time to think and I decided:

No.

Yes.

Maybe.

Yes.

She'll punch me back. Then bitch and moan about how catty girls can be.

These questions were exhausting, and exhausting is not my preferred mode of operation. The show zapped me of my auditioner's enthusiasm: I'd already auditioned for dozens of things, I'd finally achieved my goal of getting a part, and the experience—all that I'd been waiting for!—had turned out to be as glamorous as athlete's foot. So what was next? Had this production been a fluke? Was it worth it to keep trying? Well, it goes against my natural instincts to keep trying. I'm more of a quitter: When the going gets tough, I *do* get going. It's just that my brand of going takes me away from completing a goal instead of driving me ambitiously toward it. The prospect of being an actor started to look much more difficult than I had imagined, and in an effort to clear my head and gain perspective, I decided to take a couple months off from the audition circuit and review my other options. My BFA paired with my Banana Republic employment had earned me the following skill set: efficient shirt-folder, masterful Windexer (at the start of every shift I'd Windex all the mirrors in the fitting rooms). Maggie suggested that I tack on the adjective *hilarious*. Specifically, after seeing my closing-night performance in the role of Orange Girl/Sister Marthe, she'd said, "Wow. You were hilarious."

"Really?" I asked. Sister Marthe, to remind you, makes her entrance for the big, dramatic death scene. "That's not quite what I was going for."

"Well, you were." She shrugged. "You and that paper-towel habit had the audience in stitches." Maggie meant it as a compliment, but I was worried seeing as how my supposed hilarity was unintentional.

"I'm not sure that that's a good thing."

"Well, then try something where it would be. You did really well at that improv troupe audition, remember? Or what about stand-up?"

Stand-up. Interesting. Now that Maggie mentioned it, it didn't sound half bad. Another person might have seen the creative foray for exactly what it is, a horrifying chance to humiliate oneself before an audience *and*—bonus!—the only career path less stable and more difficult than acting. But I'm a renegade where practicality is concerned, so to me it sounded fun. I liked the idea of taking a break from the acting routine, all the while staying in pursuit of a goal that involved a stage, attention, and applause. And laughter! Laughter I'd encouraged!

After Maggie made the suggestion, I couldn't shake it. My parents called to ask how the acting was going, and I told them I'd switched gears.

"I'm done with acting!" I announced. "I'm trying stand-up comedy instead!"

My father was saddened by the acting abandonment though simultaneously excited about the prospect of the stand-up, and he suggested that I open with my Tina Turner impression. My mother, on the other hand, had a tougher time and started crying. "Oh god!" she wailed. "Why!? Why?! *Why* don't you try something stable! Why don't you start over? You could be a paralegal! Or a mailman! Just *please* try something where there's health insurance!"

My mother has never been a crier. I'd seen it only twice before, once when my grandfather died and once when she had to pay for an ER visit out of pocket. I found the situation very disconcerting, and I handled it by doling out the same advice she would have given me. "Let's focus on the positives!" I told her. "I don't have cancer! Now you do one."

She blew her nose and took a breath. "Well," she managed, "at least this way they'll be laughing *with* instead of *at* you. And that, I guess, is something."

10

barrel of laugh

Writing a stand-up act is no easy task. Watching Leno perform his opening monologue might convince you otherwise, but from personal experience I can say: Putting pen to paper to construct a decent punch line is good only for a headache. That, and it's an effective way to get yourself to clean; nothing prompts the urge to scour your home from floor to ceiling like staring at a blank page. I'd spend ten minutes writing in a notebook I'd titled "Funny Thoughts!" then break from my creative exploits to tackle my toilet with Ajax.

My lack of focus, skill, and originality is the only excuse I can give for what I came up with: jokes at the expense of Gwyneth Paltrow and Britney Spears (my "topical" material), in addition to tirades I'd hammered out about dating a man with the last name Hitler or, conversely, a Hasidic Jew. I wrote my Gwyneth bit around the time of the '02 Oscars, an event to which she'd worn this odd Lycra top sans brassiere.

"Is it just me . . . ?" I'd ask using an inflection I'd heard ten dozen times from other comics. "Or did Gwyneth look like she was sporting some serious FAT-BOY BOOBIES?!"

I'd shout the phrase "fat-boy boobies" like I'd offered up some nugget of comedic gold, but the audience always seemed to disagree. The notion of Gwyneth with breasts smaller than my brother's never succeeded in tickling anyone's funny bone but my own and consistently I'd leave the stage to an exhausted heckle like, "Thank *god*," or "Seriously?"

Afterward I'd sulk in the corner with an amaretto sour chased by the preferred lie of all crap comics: "It's *their* loss if they don't get me. I'm just too highbrow."

My Britney Spears joke (and this was BTF, mind you: Before the Fall) focused on a song of hers called "I'm a Slave 4 U," a three-minute masterpiece in which she talked about how much she liked to dance and have sex. There was this one line of the chorus where she sang, "I really want to spend tonight with you / I really want to do what you want me to." And from the way she performed it—the belabored exhalation, the sigh and moan that accompanied each note—you'd think she was mid-orgasm. All this hemming and hawing just because she'd donned a pair of couture underwear *over* her designer jeans? Just because she'd thrust her crotch at a muscled hip-hop dancer? It struck me as unrealistic, primarily because at this stage of her career, she still laid claim to her virginity. Well I, as a comedian, wanted to comment on this funny juxtaposition. So I'd quote the lyric to the audience: "She sings, 'I really want to spend tonight with you / I really want to do what you want me to!' Which we all know means . . ." And then my punch line, "ANAL SEX!"

I'd get the occasional seal of approval from a guy in the audience: "Anal. Totally." And one time a guy heckled after me that his girlfriend had "an asshole tighter than a baby's fist!"

You'd think a comment like that would force a joke into retirement, but no. It stayed a fixture in my repertoire, a manifestation of my comedic genius. *I'm getting the audience to reflect on their own lives,* I'd think. *I'm an artist.*

In stand-up circles, *to kill* means to do well and *to bomb* means to do poorly. That's the slang the professionals use. Performing my act once a week every week for a year, I killed just twice: once at a high school in the Bronx, and once at a midnight show in downtown Manhattan for three bachelorettes and their three dozen cohorts.

The high schoolers laughed at my eight-minute joke set not because they appreciated my cultural insights, but because in the bright cafeteria light they'd managed to see the outline of my nipples. I'd worn a thin, white T-shirt sans brassiere (à la Gwyneth) and received a look of pity and discomfort from the school's assistant principal once I got off "stage."

"Well *that* went well!" I said naively.

Before she had the chance to say, "It was your visible nipples, not your cultural commentary," a slew of rambunctious teenage boys approached me.

"I seen yer tits while you talkin'!" shouted one.

Caught off guard, I wasn't sure what to say besides "Thanks!" So that's what I did. A child said, "I seen yer tits," and I replied, "Thanks very much!"

Then he introduced himself as Lashawn and requested an autograph. "Sign that shit 'To Lashawn,'" he instructed, "'from the lady with wack nipples!'"

Never one to turn away my fan, I did as requested and signed the front of his spiral notebook, "To Lashawn from Sara Barron: the lady with wack nipples." It was the first and last time I'd be asked to sign an autograph.

My set for the bachelorettes proved more productive. These ladies were a mess of acrylic backless shirts and penis straws, and when I rambled on about Britney's proclivities for backdoor entry they went as wild as Maggie in a hospital. They were what's called my "target audience," and, as such, they found my use of words like *anal, penis, sex,* and *shit* hilarious.

Finally, I thought, *a group astute enough to understand me.*

After I'd finished my set, one of the women came over to

introduce herself. "My name is Mariah," she said, "like the singer."

Mariah was morbidly obese, and she wore a baby T that had a picture of a Buddha on the front. Beneath the Buddha was the phrase I'VE GOT THE BODY OF A GOD.

"And I wanted to tell you," she went on, "I really like your style."

"I really like *your* style," I answered back, and I meant it. The baby T, while not my favorite look on most, is a whole different ball game when worn by someone self-confident enough to laugh in the face of her own morbid obesity. I hold that sort of self-awareness in very high regard.

Mariah explained that she was a producer of "ladies' entertainment." "And I'm putting together a show that I think you'd be good for."

Dr. Phil says that opportunity is the moment when luck and hard work collide, and here, it seemed, was mine. It was neither here nor there that the first industry professional to recognize my talent was drunk and sporting a tiara. The point is that she cared to buy what I was selling—dick jokes, butt jokes, and a willingess to work for next to nothing—and that was all that mattered.

Mariah's show, she explained, was a variation on a Chippendales revue. She'd titled it *Lettin' It ALL Hang Out!* and it featured the Jewish drag sensation Ida Slapter and three male strippers. "A black guy, a white guy, and a Mexican," she told me, "so whatever flavor you want, we got!"

As far as Mariah was concerned, the show was structurally perfect except for one small missing piece: a female comedian. And she thought she'd found that missing piece in me. "Your stuff making fun of dicks and fucking's real funny," she said. "The gig's yours if you want it."

And how could I not? Before accepting a job, most people want to know details about salary, or perhaps location or schedule is a primary concern. But my checklist differs slightly: I want drag queen interaction. I want male stripper interaction. And if there's the added bonus of performing for an audience of drunk and sadly optimistic women, I'm in. I'll hop on board faster than you can say, "Sara Barron makes bad choices."

Rehearsals began the following week. The first day there I made the acquaintence of Ida and the strippers: one black, one white, one Mexican, just like Mariah promised, named Hershey's Kiss, Bootstrap Bob, and Penga, respectively. Ida served as the master of ceremonies, opening *Lettin' It ALL Hang Out!* with an imitation of the jiggly Colombian songbird Shakira, belly dancing and spoofing the performer's signature head-stuck-underwater singing style. Then she'd deep-throat a piece of produce—zucchini, cucumber, celery root; whatever was on sale at Whole Foods that week, Ida downed it like a Tootsie Roll—to get the ladies in the mood for the forthcoming buffet of multiracial genitalia.

Penga was the first of the guys to take the stage. His routine was to strip out of a business suit until he was in nothing but what's referred to by those in the male-stripper community as a "banana hammock." Then he'd mime oral sex on some lucky bride-to-be, announce her vagina to be both "nutritious and delicious," and bow to uproarious applause.

Hershey's Kiss went next. His physique was nothing to write home about, but in keeping with cultural stereotypes, his "dick," as Ida called it in his introduction, was the size of a soup can and twice as long. Like Penga, he wore a banana hammock that fit tighter than a condom. This allowed every woman in the audience, whether she sat four feet from the stage or forty, to view his strange and unusual gift. Hershey's Kiss would then spend seven minutes onstage doing anything he could to make it bounce violently around. And when it did, this sucker was of such size and consequent power that it'd knock him square against his chest on the upswing, then graze him midthigh on the return trip down.

It was my job to follow this display with a seven-minute joke set. And as it turns out, amateur jokes don't do a good job of holding an audience's attention after they've spent fifteen minutes staring at a horse cock. Up until this, my professional stage debut in Mariah Ciarullo's *Lettin' It ALL Hang Out!,* the rudest antic I'd endured while performing stand-up was a mock snoring noise. These bachelorettes had plans to change that. See, the problem with people who pay money to be entertained is that they're awfully impatient to be kept entertained. These women had spent forty bucks a head, and not for penis jokes. For penis. Actual ones attached to a Benetton ad's worth of well-endowed men, and I was an unwelcome pit stop en route to more of what they'd come for (pun intended!).

And they hated me for it.

"You suck!" they'd scream.

"Get off!"

"I hate you!" and/or "I hate you, bitch!" were other audience favorites.

We, as humans, each have our own personalized limit on how many times we can handle being told we're hated before we: a) find the wherewithal to extradite ourselves from the destructive situation, or b) learn to lean on medication. My limit is ten, and once that number came and went, I chose option B. I'd pop a Lexapro, hit the stage, and endure the scathing heckles. I did this for two months and chalked up the emotional pain and self-loathing I experienced to a simple payment of comedic dues. A comic's favorite conversation, after all, is always about how difficult comedy can be. And since so many of the professionals also take the time to medicate with store-bought booze or a bottle of meds, it seemed that all was as it should be.

Mariah, for her part, remained unaware of the disaster that unfolded every time I took the stage. She was preoccupied with Alan, the club's self-described "head bartender." Head bartender by night, he worked as a personal trainer by day and as such kept Mariah entertained with grain alcohol and flirtatious suggestions on how best to combat her obesity. "The only thing I'd do if *I* was training you personally?" he'd say. "I'd just add a little definition through your arms and midsection. Maybe a few leg lifts to tighten up those calves, but that's it. 'Cause you look good, girl. Really good."

It was both adorable and humiliating to observe their interactions. You knew Alan was in it just to try to build his client base, that if push came to shove he wouldn't touch Mariah with a bottle of Bacardi, but the sweet part was seeing her so happy, so fleetingly adored. Her face could've caught fire and she wouldn't have noticed, not as long as her "sexy baby," as she called him, remained unscathed.

Every night after I enraged the audience, Ida would return to the stage to lighten the mood with an X-rated juggling act: three dildos tossed around to the tune of Celine Dion's "My Heart Will Go On." Then by way of introducing Bootstrap Bob she'd say, "I don't know about y'all, ladies, but *my* heart goes on for big dicks! Holla!" And with that, Bob would close out the evening with an offbeat hula hoop routine: He'd masturbate until visibly aroused, then take the toy on a few goes around his own impressive endowment.

After every set at which I tried and failed, Hershey would wait backstage to comfort me. Bob and Ida still had sets to do and Penga didn't speak any English besides the phrase "nutritious and delicious," but there Hershey would be, his arms spread wide. "Sally Barron needs a hug," he'd say. (Everyone in the show called me "Sally Barron" and I went with it since bombing every night didn't do a lot to make me want to be remembered.) Then he'd hug me and I'd emerge covered in canola oil. One of the secrets I learned working alongside male strippers is that before going out onstage, they douse themselves in cooking oil—canola, preferably, as it's the most resistant to beading and provides the greatest sheen. Hershey, Penga, Bootstrap Bob, they all carried a bottle to any professional engagement, packed in their manpurse alongside a penis pump.

Penis pump?

Penis pump.

Like Santa Claus or leprechauns, I'd heard of these strange, elusive objects before but didn't think they actually existed. Not until one got tossed on the chair beside me, anyway. It looked like a hollow kazoo.

"But why?" I asked Hershey. "You don't need a penis pump."

"*Exactly*," he replied. The exchange was like one of those commercials for dandruff shampoo where someone says to a Head & Shoulders user, "But *you* don't have dandruff . . . ," and we're left to intuit that Head & Shoulders is the reason why. Ergo: Penis pumps are out there. Penis pumps work. And that simple if surprising fact is on a short list I call "Hope."

Over the course of several months, Hershey and I became good friends. It was the inevitable result of hugging on a weekly basis, of being stuck in the back corridors of a strip club with nothing else to do but interact with one another. What transpired between us was a platonic variation on the *Dirty Dancing* story line: Every night after my set, in an attempt to lift my mood and broaden my horizons, Hershey would teach me his core stripper dance moves. I learned to shake the two halves of my ass in rapid, fierce succession. I learned to shimmy, to "drop" my "junk" to the "flo." I discovered the key to an effective pelvic thrust. I practiced constantly, and this impressed Hershey, who thought I had a real gift. "Forget the comedy," he'd say, "bitch knows how to shake her shit! You're *good*!"

After three months and a marked improvement in my ability to do what's called a "whip around," Mariah finally caught wind of my comedic failings and fired. Alan had shown up to work one night with a woman named Song on his arm, and when Mariah saw them "Frenching wildly," as I used to say, she became a metaphoric pot of boiling water, ready to blow the second some asshole knocked her top off.

Next came my comedy set before the angry crowd.

With Alan preoccupied, Mariah finally had the time to watch me perform, and when she did she seemed displeased.

"WHAT THE FUCK?!" she screamed.

"Is something wrong?" I asked.

"YOU FUCKING BOMBED!" she answered. "THE REPUTA-TION *OF MY SHOW* IS ON THE LINE!"

Then she called me "pathetical" and explained (in fewer and more violent words than this) that she'd no longer be needing my services. There was no severance package, no "thank you for your contributions to the cause thus far," just a swift shove out the door and a promise from Hershey that he'd call.

He never did. But his words stayed with me: *You know how to shake your shit . . . You know how to shake your shit . . .* And then, the words he didn't say, the words he left me to intuit: *You COULD shake your shit . . . for CASH.*

But *would* I shake my shit for cash? *Could* I shake my shit for cash? Ass waxes and G-strings weren't appealing aspects, but neither was a full-time job back at Banana Republic folding shirts for eight bucks an hour. I mean, stand-up comedy sure as Sherlock wouldn't be my ticket out, unless, of course, I'd gotten on the train to chronic poverty/depression. And if that's where I was going, I'd rather take the scenic route. I'd rather amble slowly there in a pair of rhinestoned pasties.

coyote really is ugly

In the early '00s, Maggie got herself a boyfriend named Neil, whom she'd met in college; they'd bonded over a shared interest in puppetry and veganism. I liked Neil well enough, primarily because he had a third nipple that protruded so dramatically from his chest that he had to wear a Band-Aid to restrain it. And whenever he got drunk, he'd do this routine of ripping it off to mime pumping it for milk. Passing the hours in a dive bar watching a drunk man yank his pseudo-udder tickled my funny bone and fast became my favorite pastime. So when Maggie called to invite me to his twenty-fifth birthday party, I couldn't help but get excited.

"Will he milk the third nipple?" I asked. "Do you think he'll get drunk enough?"

"Yes," she said, and sighed. "I do. He told me that he wants to have the party at Coyote Ugly."

Coyote Ugly is a well-known New York bar, distinctive from the others in the city because of its unique bartending staff: They're all female, they're all clad in cowboy hats, and they all dance on the

bar in addition to the usual tending duties, e.g. opening beer, pour-
ing vodka, charging patrons, etc. These young women perform
both choreographed routines as well as free-form, improvised
grinds. I'd seen them in action, and the way it works, basically, is
that one girl is put in charge of getting drinks while the other
squats on the bar shoving her crotch toward the customers until
her thighs burn too much to keep going. When this happens, they
encourage the female patrons to get on the bar to dance along with
them. A daunting task, but one with sweet rewards, as the random
Janes who agree receive free shots and a lesbian kiss for the sole
purpose of titillating male patrons. Others are encouraged to take
off their brassieres, sign them with a Sharpie ("This bar rocks my
WORLD! xoxo Jen!"), then hang them from the rafters. This way
they can shake their chests with greater abandon and/or find joy in
returning to Coyote Ugly months or years later to find their very
own push-up/wonder something hanging lifeless but immortalized
among the hundred others. As a business venture Coyote Ugly has
been wonderfully successful, inspiring in recent years a full-length
feature film and a reality TV show on Country Music Television.
Offshoots of the New York original have opened in twelve other
U.S. cities, including Denver, Fort Lauderdale, and Las Vegas, and
these outposts sell T-shirts, hats, and thongs, all of which say COY-
OTE UGLY. And people buy them. And I know this because I see
bedecked tourists everywhere, and the experience always depresses
me more than doing stand-up comedy.

Prior to Neil's birthday party, I'd only been to Coyote Ugly
once as a college freshman and I hadn't enjoyed myself much. I'd
been forced to pay a cover charge, and for what? To watch other
women get attention? Please. There's no need to spend my parents' hard-earned money for *that,* for god's sake, when I can
streak down Fifth Avenue, my boyish tits afire, and still be less
compelling than another woman flossing. But that had been years
ago. *That* was BILTSMS: Before I Learned to Shake My Shit.
Now, things were different; now, I could envision a glorious return
wherein I, gazelle-like, leap atop the bar to join in the exploitation

extravaganza. I told Maggie to count me in for Neil's party. "I'll be there with bells on," I told her. "And way too much makeup."

A week later, a group of us gathered at midnight. The group was mostly couples: Maggie and Neil, then Neil's two best friends and both their girlfriends. I was there too, of course, and so was this other young woman named Chloe who introduced herself as Neil's cousin. Circumstances being what they were, Chloe and I spent much of the evening together, and I learned that her favorite thing to do was talk about herself. Specifically, her intimidation factor. "Guys tend to be really intimidated by me," she'd say. As a sentence, "Guys tend to be really intimidated by me" seems pretty inflexible. I mean, how many other ways are there to say it? Well, this Chloe character had a dozen variations, and it was all she cared to talk about. "They get so nervous around me" would be followed by "They're just so overwhelmed by a powerful woman, I guess," and then "A lot of guys find girls like me really, really threatening."

Girls like what? I wondered. Chloe was by no means unattractive, but she sported a FUPA bigger than a fanny pack, and her face looked strikingly like Lily Tomlin's. If she'd had a charming personality, she'd be the type you might call striking. Instead, her conversation skills just made a person suicidal.

Or, in my case, they just made a person want to dance.

I'd endured Chloe's intimidation musings for almost an hour and was in desperate search of an exit strategy when all of a sudden the Lenny Kravitz cover of the '60s smash "American Woman" came blasting through the speakers. Kravitz's rendition of "American Woman" is my favorite song to dance to (with the possible exception of Salt-n-Pepa's "Push It"). Even BILTSMS, I'd play the single and dance around my bedroom pretending my reflection in the mirror was a rival with whom I was engaged in an intense competition. There she'd be across the way, shimmying when I shimmied, grinding when I ground. She'd challenge me to dance harder, faster, better, stronger, until I arrived at my pièce de résistance: a high kick that brought me down into a split in the same moment the imaginary audience stood up to cheer for the impressive marriage of my graceful choreography and powerful athleticism.

When I hear the opening chords of "American Woman," the insistent phrase *Go Forth and Dance, Sara! Go Forth and Dance!* is quick on its heels. And circumstances depending—am I alone in my room? Or on the subway, headphones plugged into my Walkman?—I can make a cognizant decision to either indulge or ignore this impulse. But when I hear the opening chords *while* at Coyote Ugly *while* looking for an escape route from a wrenching conversation, I have no choice: I must obey.

I interrupted Chloe mid-sentence—"I'm really intimidating to guys who . . ."—by leaping deftly from my seat *at* the bar up *onto* the bar. I began with a series of hair whip-arounds and shoulder isolations.

"Oh my god!" screamed Neil. "Lookit her go!"

"Ain't no thang!" I shouted back. And it wasn't. Coordinating my shoulder isolations with a suggestive grapevine, I would not— *could* not—have been more comfortable had I been sprawled on my living room couch wrapped in a terry cloth robe. My performance was passionate yet effortless, confident yet exciting. It seemed that performing stand-up each week before a crowd of angry women had thickened my skin and afforded me a newfound fearlessness. An audience loves a fearless performer second only to the thrill of a layperson who dances like a stripper, and by the time the song ended I'd been surrounded on all sides by uproarious applause. The moment, I felt, necessitated this one move Hershey had taught me called "The Dirty Bow WOW!" It's the appropriate end to any stripper's dance routine: You drop your hands to the floor, arch your back, and—all the while angling your buttocks toward the person nearest to you—raise your chest up slowly as you return to a standing position. After that you make a peace sign *or* say "Peace out" (your choice), then walk "sexy like a wildcat" until you're off the stage.

I've entertained many fantasties over the years about the way an

audience will respond to my performances. I imagine crushing ado-
ration, but then something else occurs: I get told I have a dick, eye
contact is avoided, a day job is recommended. My dance routine to
"American Woman," on the other hand, was the single fulfillment
of those fantasies, the only occasion wherein my unrealistic expectations were not only met but surpassed, for I fielded not only the
deafening onslaught of applause, but also a job offer.

"You were amazing!" said one bartender.

"*So* amazing!" said another. "Wanna job?"

They went on to explain that one of their coworkers had
recently given her notice. "This one girl Sammy quit last week
when she booked a pilot for NBC, which was fine by us anyway,
believe me, because she danced like a retard and couldn't bartend
for shit. Point is, we need someone by Tuesday. So could you do it?
Are you interested?"

The most straightforward answer was yes. I *could* do it; I *was*
interested. I'd continued my part-time employment at Banana
Republic but was pulling in an absurdly low income, and as a
result living in a shoebox apartment and subsisting on cans of
refried beans. And watching the bartenders at Coyote Ugly sweep-
ing fives off the bar faster than you could say, "Don't you feel at
least a little like a prostitute?" led me to calculate their net worth
to be significantly higher than my own. That alone made their job
seem powerfully seductive. *I bet they go to first-run movies,* I
thought, *or get manicures someplace where they sterilize the tools.*

It also occurred to me that I'd make a lot of friends working at
Coyote Ugly. I'd endear myself to the female patrons by virtue of
having a less intimidating body than the other bartenders. They'd
consistently tell me how "refreshing" it was to see a "real" woman
with a "real" body up there on the bar. I'd be a role model turned
up in the unlikeliest of places, one who'd preach a new brand of
empowerment: Whether short or tall or fat or thin, you too can
sell yourself for money!

And I'd wind up an object of desire for countless men! "Not tonight," I'd have to tell another in a series of attractive gentlemen who'd see me from afar and want to get to know the real me, the gentle girl I kept hidden behind the wild, brusque facade. There'd be so many offers that I'd have to pick and choose. I'd have to give excuses like, "I'm just needing some time to myself right now," or "I'm actually seeing someone at the moment."

The more I thought about it, the clearer it became that bartending at Coyote Ugly was the obvious key to wealth, companionship, and notoriety. And in that moment, with my cheeks still flushed from dancing, with the sound of people clapping still ringing in my ears, the only thing more seductive than earning lots of money each time I stuffed myself into a cowboy hat and low-rise jeans was the prospect of a nightly round of applause. That kind of validation is a very big deal for an average exhibitionist like me. Especially when you're fresh off two months of incisive, nightly heckles, the chance for nightly applause seems like heaven. *Heaven* and *cowboy hat* aren't words I ever thought I'd use so close together, but sometimes you round a corner that was unforeseen. Sometimes the God of Lowbrow Entertainment closes a door (you're fired from telling penis jokes) but then opens a window somewhere else, and you get the chance to bare yourself through quasi-naked dance.

I told the bartender I was available.

"MISTAKE!" roared a voice. "BIG MISTAKE!"

But whose? Had I heard it in my head? Was it the God of Lowbrow Entertainment? My mother? Or Maggie?

Maggie. She'd sneaked up behind me during my conversation with the bartender and cared to offer an opinion. "It's a goddamn slut parade in here," she said. "Not a place to get a job. That's a horrible idea."

The "Horrible Idea" rationale has never been one to deter me. On the contrary, I have a knack for the follow-through of horrible ideas. High-risk as they are, I prefer to focus on the sliver of potential for a payback. *Sure, I might degrade myself among the slut parade,* I think, *but what if—just if!—I'm regaled with applause and phone numbers instead!* Whatever the cost of my failings, I rationalize the risk by saying it will be worth it for the story.

"It will be worth it for the story," I told Maggie. "What's the worst that could happen?"

"Where do I start?" she asked. "*That* woman"—and she pointed to the bartender who'd offered me the job—"is wearing sunglasses. Indoors. And I'm pretty sure that she's the boss."

"Well, that's just more fodder for a funny story," I rationalized. "And besides, you're being judgmental. I think she seems nice."

"No you don't," Maggie countered. "You just like her because she likes your dancing. There's a difference. And my point is that she seems dangerous: Spend a month with her, and you'll wind up just another asshole in a baby T."

"How can you say that?"

"I can say it 'cause it's true."

When your friends don't tell you what you want to hear, I think it's important to ignore them. Here, I wrote Maggie off with an exasperated, "Oh, *whatever,*" and two days later headed in for my first Coyote Ugly training session. I wore jeans and a tube top that I'd purchased specifically for the occasion at Strawberry, a store specializing in clothing that makes women look like they'll have unprotected sex, all for the bargain price of $12.99. I looked cheap in every sense, save for a pair of New Balance sneakers, which were excellent for dancing.

The bartender with the sunglasses greeted me at the door and introduced herself as Jesse. We exchanged pleasantries, and just as I'd begun reflecting on how lovely she seemed despite the sunglasses misstep, she launched into a memorized speech regarding the hardships of life as a "Coyote."

"People think being a Coyote is all fun and games," she said, "but it's really hard work. I wanna be clear with you about that from the get-go."

Just as Banana Republic employees will refer to the store as "Banana," the women of Coyote Ugly refer to themselves as

"Coyotes." They'll begin a sentence, "As a Coyote . . . ," or quickly interject with, "It's 'cause I'm a Coyote!" In my first five minutes there, I heard Jesse say, "Last week my friend and I went dancing, and I saw this girl across the bar and I just *knew*: I was like, '*That* is a Coyote.' And it turned out she was! She worked at the bar in Tampa! How crazy is that? I thought it was crazy!"

As a Coyote, the first task I found difficult was calling myself a Coyote. I couldn't muster the same unironic enthusiasm as the other girls. And according to Jesse, I also had trouble composing an outfit.

"What you're wearing won't work," she said.

"Are you sure?" I asked. "I bought it at Strawberry. I thought it'd be perfect."

"The shirt's too long," she explained. "As a Coyote you've got to show your skin from here"—she indicated an inch beneath her breasts—"to here"—and pointed to an inch above where another woman's pubic hair would be, where Jesse's *would've* been if she hadn't shaved herself to within an inch of looking like a five-year-old. The lighting at Coyote Ugly was shoddy, but still, if glanced from the appropriate angle, you could see her stubble growing in. An appetizing touch, I thought, to get her patrons in a drinking mood.

I was personally opposed to exposing my torso from breast to hip. It wasn't an issue of modesty, I just didn't want to look naive. I didn't want to elicit the response, "Does she *know* what she looks like?" I may have trimmed my FUPA down (the anxiety caused by post-collegiate life—earning money, paying bills, understanding the ways in which mine was a meaningless existence—had been good for significant weight loss, if nothing else), but that didn't make me bikini-ready. I didn't see the correlation between saddlebag exposure and increased alcohol sales. "It's not the best look for me," I told Jesse, but to no avail. She was already tucking the bottom ten inches of my Strawberry tube top under the wire of the shirt's own built-in bra.

"Rule Number One about being a Coyote," she began—this was

125

the first in a series she'd reveal to me over the course of the evening—"is that there's no room for insecurity behind the bar. You're a strong, sexy woman. And if you don't show the customers who's in control straight outta the gate, they'll eat you alive."

There was a gentleman at the end of the bar ready to make good on her promise. Six feet tall by three feet wide, he wore one of those American flag pins that ran rampant on lapels from '01 to '03, except he'd pinned his to the enormous sports jersey he had on that read, HATED BY MANY, WANTED BY PLENTY, DISLIKED BY SOME, BUT CONFRONTED BY NONE! He eyed my now-exposed midriff and said, "You look good." Admittedly, I was flattered by his comment, until he followed up the phrase by saying, ". . . with all that meat on your bones."

"That's Len," said Jesse, "he's the sweetest. He hangs out here every night to protect us from the weirdos." The insinuation that Len himself wasn't a "weirdo" was even more disconcerting than the sensation of my visible torso. He continued to shower me with compliments, all of which made reference to me as a sort of food, from the banal ("You look good enough to eat!") to the creative ("Your belly looks sweeter than a cupcake!"). I kept looking to Jesse for confirmation that what Len had said was disconcerting, but all I got was "*So* sweet, right?" before she ran back to the storage room to fetch me a cowboy hat. "Now you can dance!" she declared. "Rule Number Two of being a Coyote: You can't dance without a cowboy hat!"

"Right now?" I asked. "You want me to dance right now?"

I'd felt comfortable atop the bar at midnight on a Friday when the place was packed with drunken, half-clothed maniacs. But this was 5:30 on a Tuesday. You could have heard a pin drop. The music was barely audible and the bar was nearly empty save for Len, this other person of indeterminate gender asleep in the corner with a shopping cart, and two men over fifty, both in business suits.

Jesse nodded. "Rule Number Three of being a Coyote is that you don't dance when you *want* to dance, you dance when you *have* to dance." She swatted at my ass with the cowboy hat, an action she intended as a sort of "giddyup!" equivalent, I think. "Now go practice on Len."

Len made another allusion to eating me, something like "Don't be afraid; I won't bite," or maybe it was "I won't bite, unless you want me to." The point is, the words were less memorable than the action with which they were accompanied. Once I'd started my bump and grind to the faint sound of a Whitesnake song underscored by the heavy breathing of the customers, Len began pulling at the waistband of my underwear (it was made ripe for the snapping thanks to my makeshift half shirt) and stuffing dollar bills into it. This annoyed me: If I had to be manhandled, then *at least* I wished to be well compensated.

"Hey, Len," I said, "make it a five instead of a single, will ya? Mama needs a brand new bag." I meant it as a lighthearted articulation of a genuine sentiment, but it succeeded only in irritating Jesse into an explanation of Rule Number Four of being a Coyote.

"As a Coyote," she explained, "you're not allowed to dispute tips with a customer. It's considered *really* tacky."

This was a hard sentence to take seriously from a woman in a halter top that read, FUCK MILK. GOT POT? but I didn't care to argue. I apologized as a means to avoid conflict and started to climb down off the bar.

"No! Stay where you are," she squealed. "While you're up there, you might as well practice Rule Number Five: Tequila Shot Coyote Style."

A shot of tequila downed in the "style" of a "Coyote" was a move I'd seen performed on Neil at his birthday party without having known its name. An intricate if atypical pas de deux, this particular mode of tequila consumption involved the Coyote seating a male patron atop the bar, and with his back now toward her, she'd stand on the bar above him and pin his shoulders between her knees. Next, she'd pour a cup of tequila straight from the bottle into her mouth, then spit it directly from her mouth into his. From the outside, it looked like a sure way to get drunk or oral

herpes, and Rule Number Five was that a given Coyote perform
this feat six times a night to rile up the crowd. Rule Number Six
was that she practice prior to performance. And Rule Number
Seven was that my first practice session be on Len.

"Hey, cutie!" Jesse called to him. "Sara's coming over so she can
practice Tequila Shot Coyote Style!"

There's a big discrepancy between my tolerance for emotional
pain versus my tolerance for physical pain. I'll indulge a moment
of perspective and admit that I haven't ever *really* been tested in
either department—a breakup in '05 and the removal of a plantar
wart in '98 have topped the lists in both respective categories—
but over the course of my lifetime I've learned that physical pain I
can handle, and emotional pain I cannot: I get choked up if someone says "excuse me" too harshly on the subway. My stand-up
attempts demolished the only shred of self-confidence I had
maintained, forced me into a jittery Lexapro dependency, and in a
moment skewed by the afterglow of a well-received performance,
I'd thought Coyote Ugly could be the thing to bolster me back up.
When I realized the daily grind would instead involve a smear of
Len's meat-scented saliva, my survivalist instinct kicked in. *You
simply cannot do that,* I thought. *You won't survive the degradation.* So when Jesse urged me toward him, I froze. She looked back
at me expectantly.

"You know," I said, and I giggled to lighten the mood, to give
the impression that ours was just a breezy conversation between
friends, "that *does* seem like it'd be, um, helpful. The practicing, I
mean."

"You best be sure as shit it is," said Len. "You best hold me with
those cupcake knees and gimme my tequila!"

What *in the world* was with the cupcake metaphors? Len
clunked his half-ton frame atop the bar, opened his mouth, and
flicked his tongue at me aggressively, a sort of physical double
entendre, I'd guessed, intended to demonstrate his enthusiasm
both for tequila *and* for oral sex. I appreciate a man who appreciates performing oral sex, but when measured against his date-

rape potential, his sports jersey, and his flag pin, it wasn't enough to keep me interested.

"Oh, okay!" I said. "That sounds great! But would you mind if first I went outside for a cigarette break?" I didn't smoke, but I needed an excuse to leave, and "cigarette break" sounded viable. I imagined Rule Number Eight of being a Coyote was that you smoked to raise your coolness quotient.

"Sure," said Jesse. "Go smoke your cig, then once you come back we'll rehearse the tequila shot with Len, and I'll teach you the dance routine to 'Pour Some Sugar on Me'! Oh! And do you need a bigger cowboy hat? I didn't realize how big your head was."

I told her I thought a bigger cowboy hat was probably a good idea, then patted my back pocket as though to indicate that that's where I stocked my nicotine. I laid my too-snug cowboy hat atop the bar and walked out the door. Once I saw Jesse head back to the stockroom to fetch a bigger hat, and once Len seemed preoccupied with repositioning his testicles against his barstool, I ran for the subway. It took a few minutes before I was safely underground, and I had to field a couple heckles along the way since I'd forgotten to untuck the bottom of my tube top. Someone shouted, "How much an hour?" at First Avenue and Eleventh Street, and that was followed by, "Slow down, sexy, sloooooooow dooooooown!" at First and Fourteenth.

So I untucked my tube top *from* my tube top, leaned against the wall, and waited for the train. The sense of loss I felt at having abandoned my Coyote Ugly dream was mitigated by the accompanying sense of relief. I'd have to say good-bye to the fantasy of first-run movies, but at least I wouldn't have to wake one morning to realize I now made comfortable reference to myself as a Coyote. At least I had not become adjusted to makeshift bikini top as work uniform. Besides, what good would the extra cash have done me, *really*? Sure there'd be the aforementioned movies, and perhaps I could've upgraded to brand-name shampoo, but most of all I'd wanted to impress my parents. I wanted to prove I was financially self-sufficient and imagined that come Hanukkah, I'd surprise my mother with a cashmere scarf instead of my usual gift of store-bought cheesecake. Well, standing there I realized just how stupid this course of action would have been. My parents know all about my limited skill set, and if I ever bought my mom a cashmere scarf, she'd want to know exactly how I'd found the money.

"Coyote Ugly," I'd answer. This phrase would mean nothing to her, so she'd run to the nearest computer to Google it, take one look at their website, and convince herself that I had herpes. My mother is an educated woman—she knows herpes are for keeps—and I could never put her through that. I knew there had to be another way to make some decent money. Perhaps I'd find a job involving corporate dress and fax machines. Or I'd use my three hours spent as a Coyote as the basis for my next spoken-word performance piece. I could be discovered, you know, and it could become the next long-running, Off Broadway smash. Sort of like Blue Man Group but without the blue men. Or the group. I might also win the lottery.

In the moment, the possibilities seemed endless and the only thing I knew for sure was this: I needed a shower. And a baggy, long-sleeve shirt.

hombres

1 2

the actors

My friends are divided into two groups: One is successful in their love lives but unsuccessful in their careers; the other has impressive careers but no romantic lives to speak of. Then there are two of us who don't fit neatly into either group. First, my friend Kate. Kate runs a successful catering business serving overpriced finger foods to hedge-funders *and* she's married to a man who looks like John Stamos. As her friend, I'm privy to certain details of her marriage, like the fact that they still have sex three times a week after five years together and, more impressive still, that for their last anniversary he purchased *and installed* a washer-dryer. That's not something that happens often in New York City, but it did for Kate since her life's perfect.

At the other end of the spectrum, there's me. My "career" has revolved around minimum wage in retail sales. And while Kate keeps busy spooning a Stamos look-alike, I've spent my time dating actors. Musical theater actors mostly, with a couple straight ones thrown in for good measure. I've convinced myself that said pattern isn't my fault, that my dad's the one to blame for having instilled in me the sense that straight men should enjoy the nuances of Sondheim.

ONE DAY I arrived at an audition for a spoken-word version of the 1960s musical *Hair,* where I met a young man named Matthew. Matthew and I literally bumped into each other while rehearsing "Aquarius," the required audition "song." (I use the quotation marks because it wasn't really a song the way it was going to be presented in this particular production. It was instead a spoken-word piece that went: "WHEN the moon . . . when THE mooon . . . when the MOOOOON . . . when SHE is in the SEVENTH HOUSE! The what? The SEVENTH HOUSE!" etc.) We'd both been using our hands emphatically, a spoken-word performance crutch I'd picked up watching the professional "poets" on HBO's *Def Poetry Jam,* when ours collided in an inadvertent high five. We both yelped in pain.

"Well," said Matthew, "I guess that's what we get for doing spoken word."

Part of maturing as an artist involves getting over spoken word as a tolerable means of expression. Like crack or Christina Aguilera, it's fine to like it when you're twenty, but as you creep toward thirty, it's just embarrassing. Spoken word has been my guilty pleasure for way too long, and as a result, I feel connected to the other people out there who equally hate to love it.

After the audition, Matt and I went to the nearest pharmacy to get ice packs for our wrists.

"Geez." Matt winced. "I think I might've sprained mine."

"I sprained my wrist once," I said, "from excessive masturbation."

A lady takes a risk by being this forward, so *thank god* Matt responded positively. He laughed and blushed and said, "Wow. That's hilarious." And then he asked me on a date.

"I've got tickets to see *Cabaret* this week," he said, "and John

Stamos is in it. That *Full House* guy, you know? He's supposed to be pretty good."

"John Stamos?" I asked. "In person?"

Matt nodded. "I've got tickets for Thursday if you're free."

John Stamos is, in my opinion, the most flawless man who has ever lived. The rest of the broads out there can have their Pitts and Clooneys, but I'll take Stamos every time. Mine is a steadfast allegiance that began in 1986, and the opportunity to see him in person was the best thing to ever happen to me. It *was* the best thing to ever happen to me until the night of my date with Matthew rolled around and after the show *John Stamos signed my* Playbill *and our forearms rubbed together!* I got diarrhea in response. Not immediately, but basically what happened was that the excitement of the moment overwhelmed me. Stamos contact occurred, I screamed, pranced absurdly around, knocked something out of whack internally, and then was hit with that unmistakable gastrointestinal message that says, *Hey, lady!* I'm *the one in charge!*

So I told Matt I needed a ladies' room and since the theater was already locked up, we went to a nearby T.G.I. Friday's.

I spent a half hour stuck in the bathroom. Awkward as it was when I finally emerged, Matt behaved like the perfect gentleman. "You poor thing," he said, "are you okay?" I was pale and perspiring and there were flecks of toilet paper I'd used to blot my sweat still stuck to my forehead. Matt graciously removed them. "Toilet paper," he muttered, and flicked them discreetly to the ground. "Let's get you a ginger ale, shall we?"

He flagged down a waitress to order a ginger ale for me and an appletini for himself, then settled into the banquette. "So," he said conspiratorially, "how hot is John Stamos?"

I both understand and appreciate that some straight men drink appletinis. And I understand and appreciate that some straight men comfortably refer to other men as being hot; it's part of their shtick of sensitivity and über-hipness. But *both*—"Can I get an appletini?" *plus* "How hot is John Stamos?"—these actions scream *gay* louder than a strap-on strapped on Missy Elliott.

Now, for me personally, homosexuality in a boyfriend isn't a deal breaker. Neither is it my preferred mode of operation, but my point is I can swing it if I have to, most especially because I like having sex in the dark. *Brokeback Mountain* suggested to Middle Americans everywhere that gay men who have sex with women do so from behind. But (pun intended!) speaking from personal experience with Matthew the Musical Theater Actor, I can say that the more consistent thread is pitch-black bedrooms. Every time we had sex (which, from the get-go, averaged in at less than once every two weeks . . . *and* we'd just met . . . *and* we were both twenty-two), we did so in Matt's windowless box of a bedroom, shielded from the light and the reality that neither one of us was screwing Stamos. We made it last for six months, a stretch of relationship success we enjoyed no thanks to my friends, who badgered me constantly with questions that I didn't care to answer.

"Your boyfriend is a homosexual," said Maggie, "which is *fine*. I just want to know *you* know."

I scoffed and toed my usual line, which was to tell her she was being judgmental. "He's not gay, he's nice," I'd said. "Matt's just a nice guy who enjoys musical theater. Shame on you for stereotyping."

Of course a statement like this is an invitation to the God of Denial to have a laugh at your expense. The day after this tête-à-tête between Maggie and me, I had plans with Matt to rent a movie. We chose the Tori Spelling I've-matured-as-an-actress vehicle *Trick*, a film about two gay men trying to find a place to have sex. Oh! *And* about how Tori Spelling has matured as an actress. Anyway, toward the beginning of the film there's this highly erotic hombre/hombre massage scene, over the course of which my boyfriend Matt sprouted an erection. Well, it wasn't 1992 anymore and I knew that an erection meant "I'd *Like* to Have Sex" not "I *Can't* Have Sex." And I knew the source of inspiration didn't have to do with me or Tori Spelling, but rather the rubbing of hands on shaven chests and oddly muscled derrieres. And he knew I knew, which meant we'd reached the point of no return: There could be no more denial.

So we both feigned headaches—"Oh my god, you, too? That's weird!"—exchanged a bone-dry peck on the lips, and called it a night. We never spoke again after that. This was a bizarre and dramatic choice on both our parts considering we'd been dating for months. I suppose it was just our way of dealing with how traumatic we'd both thought our final night to be. It was also a shame: Matt was always so nice and possessed such a nuanced perspective on spoken-word poetry, and never in my life before or since have I met someone so tender when confronted with another person's diarrhea. I'll always remember him for that. And I'll always hold out hope to one day see him strolling arm in arm with some bossy bottom of a gent, flushed with a postcoital glow I could never have provided.

I MET WILL Glazer through my (openly) gay friend Mike. Mike and I worked together at Banana Republic and formed a friendship based upon mutual hatred: Neither one of us could stand our Banana Republic coworkers, who described their job to those who asked as "working in fashion." It was a euphemism too pathetic for either one of us to handle.

Mike worked at Banana Republic because he'd made the same mistake I had and majored in theater in college. That's where he met Will Glazer, who, unlike either of us, now had a successful acting career: He traveled the country working in childrens' theater. At the time of our meeting, Will was in New York enjoying a few months off after closing a Cleveland production of *Hansel and Gretel,* and Mike wanted desperately for me to meet him. "I've had fantasies about Will for years," he confessed, "so I was hoping you'd have sex with him *for me,* and then report back."

I considered the proposition and decided, *Why not?* A girl only lives once after all.

Mike was thrilled when I agreed. "Oh my god!" he screamed. "Really?! I was only half serious! You'd really do it?"

"Sure," I said. "I have no one else on my itinerary." This wasn't entirely true. The higher-ups at Banana Republic had recently hired a dashing maintenance man from Nicaragua, and I entertained many afternoon fantasies of a cross-cultural throw down amid the mops and Windex bottles in the storage room. But I didn't care to count my chickens before they hatched. Or, to get more specific about it, to bank on a janitor I saw once a week who referred to me as Sandra.

"Oh my god!" Mike screamed again, and clapped his hands together. "This is fantastic! He'll be *so* fun in bed I bet! Will's such an awesome dancer!"

It's a myth that good dancers are also good in bed. I'm a great dancer, but I'm also self-absorbed and lazy. And the latter aspects outweigh the former in terms of their influence over my bedroom persona.

"That's a false correlation," I explained, "so let's both of us approach this project with lowered expectations."

Mike agreed to try, and one week later I met Will. It was summer, so we convened at this lovely outdoor beer garden, drank to excess to make the conversation more comfortable, then headed back to my place under the guise of watching *A Chorus Line*. Around beer number five, we'd stumbled upon the coincidence that it was our mutually favorite musical, so it had felt natural enough for me to say, "Oh my god! That's *my* favorite musical! I own the Michael Douglas version on VHS. Let's go back to my place and watch it!"

This approach allowed me to feel a little less like a sexual predator and, more to the point, to repress the prostitutey element of the situation. See, if I successfully bagged Will and spared no detail in my report back, Mike had promised to buy me this beautiful cashmere sweater at Banana Republic. This sweetened the pot of the pursuit but also meant I'd be having sex for material gain—which, regardless of whether or not you've had a Bat Mitzvah or received your BFA, I'm pretty sure qualifies as prostitution. Now on the one hand, if I ended up liking Will enough that I would've done it anyway, I was in the moral clear. But on the other hand, the whole Coyote Ugly experience had unfolded just two months prior and I'd planned for that to be my *singular* walk along the line of prostitution. I wasn't in the market for another. I *was* in the market for a new cashmere sweater, however, which is what made it all so complicated.

Such were the thoughts in my head prior to my date with Will Glazer, which is why I was thrilled to get him back to my place just by saying, "I own the Michael Douglas version on VHS!"

It's what came next that proved disastrous.

The problems surrounding the, ahem, romantic part of our evening are two I'll label first "The Seduction Technique" and second "The Body Dysmorphia," as this is the order in which they occurred.

THE SEDUCTION TECHNIQUE

Once we got back to my apartment, Will threw me forcefully onto the couch (a promising beginning!), but then instead of joining me there he leaned against the wall on the opposite side of the living room.

"Now check *this* out," he purred. Then he pas de bourréd at me.

A pas de bourré (pronounced *pa-da-boo-ray*), is a dance move, the French name for a triplet—step side, step back, step front—performed in community-theater musical productions all across the country. Will performed them *at* me, all the way across my living room floor. And as he did so he kept asking, "You like this? Yeah? You like this?"

I found this course of action problematic. First, the pas de bourré itself, which felt as masculine as a vagina. Second, the narrative that overscored it. Reminiscent of when Elijah told me, "Do your thing, girl! Pee on me!" I didn't appreciate having to shoulder the burden of someone else's fetish. It's *your* thing that you pee or pas de bourré. And these absurd references, the questions or statements to suggest *my* unearned interest—"You like this? Yeah?"—their attempts to seduce are counterproductive.

THE BODY DYSMORPHIA

Will had a penis the size of an engorged clitoris. No. That's not fair. I should say that Will had a penis that was *closer in size* to an engorged clitoris than it was to an average-sized penis. And to add fuel to the fire of his situation, he didn't seem to know it. Will was a talker, and while having sex he asked repeatedly, "Too deep?" "Feel good?" "Right there?" "Like that?" or "*You* like that?" The questions were terribly ironic. I had no idea what to say, and so as the sex went on, I settled on humming: one long, continuous sound I hoped he'd interpret as a general answer to everything he seemed to want to talk about.

A penis like a light switch I can handle, but a lack of self-awareness I cannot. Once asked, "Too deep?" I knew Will and I would never work. And it was just as well seeing as how he'd be leaving in a month to go play Rolf in *The Sound of Music* at some theater in Poughkeepsie.

My coworker Mike, on the other hand, wasn't going anywhere. The next day at work he was chomping at the bit for details. "So?" he asked. "Was he wild?"

I nodded.

"Aggressive?"

"Yes."

"And . . . ?" Mike took a deep breath and gestured toward his own khaki-covered crotch.

"Spectacular," I answered, "a double-stacked soup can if ever I've seen one."

What good would an honest answer have done? This way Mike was happy and my conscience was free from the burden of having revealed Will's secret.* He'd done me no wrong, after all. Well, I mean I *had* been pas de bourréd at, but betraying so personal a detail as a means of revenge? That just seemed unfair.

Then as promised, Mike gave me the hard-won cashmere sweater. Did this make me a hooker? Hooker-ish? Perhaps. But seeing as how I hadn't squealed on the part that really mattered, I hoped to qualify as one who had a heart of gold.

ONE DAY I was walking down the street in a pair of high-heeled sandals when I tripped and fell and skinned my palms. A young man dashed immediately to my side to ask if I was all right.

"I work as a hand model," he said.

I thought he'd follow up with something like, "So here's an expensive healing salve I just so happen to have on me." But instead he said, "And whenever I see someone wipe out like you just did, I think, *Oh man, that could've been me!*"

I'm more sympathetic than most to the profoundly self-involved. I both identify with and understand their shortcomings and, in so doing, hope to avoid the pitfall of hypocrisy.

The young man introduced himself as Josh. Josh helped me to my feet and asked me out for a drink. A drink sounded nice. See, I'd donned my high-heeled sandals that afternoon so as to look sexy to this guy who worked at my local dry cleaners, but when I got there to pick up my stuff, it turned out to be his day off. Just

---

*I *did* just give away Will's secret, didn't I? Here's why: Three years after our romantic interlude, Will ended up back in New York dating a friend of mine named Sue. They were together two years, lived together for one. Will cheated on Sue repeatedly, a fact she was made privy to only after contracting gonorrhea while in a seemingly monogamous relationship. How? From whom? Mr. I-Can't-Keep-My-Engorged-Clitoris-of-a-Penis-in-My-Pants is who. Well, just after giving Sue gonorrhea, Will decided it was time to leave her. And I simultaneously decided that it wasn't my responsibility to keep the problem of his privates private anymore.

my luck. Anyway, this is why in the moment of meeting Josh I'd been feeling very all-dressed-up-and-nowhere-to-go. So I told him, "Sure," and we walked to a nearby bar, ordered a couple beers, and got to know each other better.

"I'm an actor," said Josh. "Commercials mostly. And then I do the hand modeling thing on the side."

"Me, too," I said. "I mean, I don't hand model"—and I offered a quick flash of my man-paws—"but I'm an actor, too." Josh wanted to know if he might have seen me in anything recently. "Not unless you shop at Banana Republic or spent last month in Hoboken," I answered. "But I've got a callback this week for a production of *Peter Pan* at a midtown senior center. You?"

"I booked a commercial for Staples last month."

I clinked my beer to his. "Well here's to that!" I said. "Congrat-ulations!"

"Thanks," he said. "I was lucky. I made a shitload of cash off it."

That's when we decided to settle up our bar tab, and Josh asked to borrow money. "Oh shit!" he said. "I just realized I've got, like, zero cash on me. Can you spot me this time? The next one'll be on me, I swear." The insinuation that there would even be a next one between me and an honest-to-goodness commercial actor/part-time hand model got me excited, so I gave him the benefit of the doubt on the empty wallet, slapped a twenty on the bar, and offered up my number.

Nowadays successful commercial actors—those lucky few who hit the jackpot of being overcompensated for their "art"—impress me as much as a potty-trained eighteen-year-old. But I was younger when I met Josh, less embittered, more enamored of anyone who'd enjoyed the faintest sprinkle of success. I liked that his company felt glamorous, and he liked that I was delusional enough to think that his company felt glamorous. These affec-tions sustained an eight-month relationship. Over the course of our time together, I learned that Josh's favorite pastime was to talk about how much money he made versus how little money he had. He'd book a commercial and then, feeling flush, burn it all in a matter of weeks. He'd buy designer clothes, designer skin care, designer sushi, and so on, until he was penniless again, back to begging for someone else to buy his beers or spot him on his cell phone bill. It was an irritating quality, but the perks of his hand modeling career made it worth dealing with: Josh got manicures frequently and so had amassed dozens of coupons for free companion manicures, and he gave them all to me. These were good manicures, too, the spa kind that would otherwise have run me twenty bucks a pop. My man-claws looked fantastic, and that's a hard thing to just up and walk away from, seeing as how a lady gets adjusted to a lifestyle. Josh and I were completely incompatible in every other way. He mooched more fiercely than an infant and spoke incessantly about "the business." His value system turned my stomach faster than a can of pig's feet stuffed in gelatin. *But*. The women at the nail salon did this shiatsu thing during the massage portion of my manicures that made it worth enduring a man who called himself "an up-and-comer."

"As an up-and-comer," Josh had said once over brunch, "you start to feel the pressure—you really do."

"The pressure to what?" I asked. I had no idea what he was talking about.

"You know, like, top yourself."

Josh had just wrapped a two-line role in a Febreze commercial. "You mean you feel a pressure to top your performance in that Febreze commercial?" I asked. "Is that what you're talking about?"

"Totally," he answered. And then, having dug into his wallet, he said, "Oh, shit! I'm out of cash. Can you buy brunch?"

I wish I could say that such financial indiscretions forced me into dumping him, but he dumped me before I got around to it. He'd made the decision to move from New York to Los Angeles and didn't care to try our relationship long distance. "As an up-and-comer," he explained, "I realize I have to put my career first. And L.A. is where the work is."

I had it coming, frankly. It's true he mooched me nearly out of house and shoebox home, but that still didn't justify dating a man solely for cuticle maintenance and shiatsu massage. Do that, and you must brace yourself for a helping of bad karma: I used him, so he dumped me, so we were even. Fine.

But then Josh made the mistake of bouncing the ball back into my court.

Not long after our breakup—a point at which I'd pictured him in L.A. hustling between auditions as he tried to outdo his Febreze performance—Josh wandered into my Banana Republic arm in arm with his new girlfriend. (I based this assessment on some in-my-face hand holding.) He looked surprised to see me there, which was idiotic seeing as how he knew it's where I worked, and which I can't account for except to say that what Josh lacked in callused palms he also lacked in reasoning skills.

"Oh," he mumbled when he saw me standing slack-jawed in the jean department.

"I thought you were moving to L.A.," I said.

"Well, I *was*," he answered, and his voice got this defensive edge. Like it was my fault he'd brought his new girlfriend into his old girlfriend's job. "But then I met Natalia. And anyway, well, I didn't know you *still* worked here."

"I do."

"Got it. Geez. All right. So . . . how's the acting going?"

If I date you for your free companion manicures and you dump me, so be it. But do *not* mock my retail career and acting failures in front of the new girlfriend you've chosen to shove down my throat. "What goes around comes all the way back around," are the immortal words of Justin Timberlake, and I believe them. I also believe that you're pinning a shit magnet on your forehead if you, an actor, mock the failings of another. On this point, I'm correct. Two years would pass before I saw Josh again. I'd be on vacation in L.A. enjoying a stroll down the Third Street Promenade. I'd be window shopping, admiring the wrap dresses I thought could work best at creating an hourglass shape, when suddenly there would be Josh. Inside the Gap. Working as a greeter.

"Hey there!" he'd say to everyone who entered. "How're you doing today?"

Honestly, I thought I heard angels sing when I first saw him standing there, then realized it was just the flush of happiness combined with the Sarah McLachlin song I'd been listening to on my CD Walkman. If I was someone less adept at holding grudges, I would've let the sight of him suffice. But woulda coulda shoulda. I fluffed my bangs and walked on in.

"HEY THERE!" I shouted.

Josh was shocked to see me. "WHOA!" he shouted back. "Hey. What are *you* doing here? Did you move to L.A.?"

"Nope!" I answered. "I'm just on vacation. But enough about me. What's up with you? How's the acting going?"

"Great," Josh said, sounding strained. "Really great. I got a call-back last week for a Colgate commercial. Hopefully that'll come through since this greeter stuff is just, you know, temporary."

"Right." I nodded. "Sure it is."

I stuck around just long enough to hear him get yelled at by his manager for fraternizing, then said good-bye and walked to the Jamba Juice next door to get myself a smoothie. Jamba Juice has such wonderfully uplifting names for their drinks: "Strawberry Nirvana." "Carribean Passion." "Peach Pleasure." And sipping my "Peach Pleasure" on this sunny California day, I knew why: I sipped peach. And I felt pleasure.

| 3

the clown

The other week I was waiting for the subway at Union Square. It was late at night and I was reading *The New York Times,* which, for me, always means I'm in a position to be easily distracted. Concentrating on world affairs is always something I feel I *should* do, which means I *do* do it, but only occasionally and always poorly. So I was people-watching and glancing intermittently around the station when all of a sudden I caught the eye of a man in a clown outfit. He winked at me and started walking in my direction. I'm not usually the type to talk to strangers—especially one in a red foam nose who initiates an interaction with a wink— but this guy looked really familiar, which piqued my interest because it's not like I know all that many working clowns in the city. You'd think if I saw one who looked familiar, my next thought would be, *Oh, right* . . . that *guy.* But that was not the case. I knew I knew him and I couldn't figure out how, so I decided to say hello and he, a well-mannered clown, said hello back.

"I think we've met before," I said. "Remind me of your name."

He bowed then and did a *ta-da!* with his hands before saying, "I'm Mr. Clown!"

It was a spectacular introduction, so I laughed and said, "All right, 'Mr. Clown.' But what's your *real* name?"

I expected a reply along the lines of "Don't you remember?" I'd be embarrassed and shake my head no and he'd continue, "I'm so-and-so! From such-and-such! Well, I'm a street performer now!" Then we'd have a laugh, talk about how much time had passed, exchange numbers, and make an empty promise to catch up over coffee.

But instead Mr. Clown said again, "I'm Mr. Clown!"

So *again* I asked his real name.

"I just told you: Mr. Clown. That *is* my real name."

"Well, I don't believe you," I told him.

He shrugged. "You don't have to believe Mr. Clown; it's still my real name."

Talking in the third person is even more bizarre than titling oneself a clown in my opinion, so I shouted, "Who are YOU?! Now answer, 'I am . . .'"

". . . MR. CLOWN!"

The other people on the subway platform started taking notice as I racked my brain for more specific possibilities.

"Are you Josh Green?" I asked. "From Sunset Woods Day Camp?"

"Nope."

"Sam Feinzimer?"

"Nope."

"Are you from Chicago? New York? Did we go to school together?"

My gut instinct was that I'd seen him naked at some point in the last decade, but I couldn't be too sure, so I continued listing names: "Danny Levinson?"

"I *am* Mr. Clown!"

"Justin Rubenstein?"

"I *am* Mr. Clown!"

After five minutes he tired of our back-and-forth and excused himself by heading to the nearest, fullest garbage can. "I need new props," he said, and rummaged through until he found a Poland Spring bottle, a Coke can, and a container of baby powder.

"Watch this!" he declared. "I can juggle!"

For me, voluntary contact with garbage and dementia are tightly intertwined. The sight of the rummaging knocked me out of my trance of frustration and I thought, *So you're mistaken. He's not someone you know; he just looks like he is.* But then once I'd found the wherewithal to turn to go, he taunted me with, "Why are you leaving so soon . . . SARA . . . BARRON?"

One thing I knew for sure was that I hadn't given him my name.

"WHO *ARE* YOU?!" I bellowed.

"MR. CLOWN!" he answered back. "It was lovely seeing you again!" And with that, he waved good-bye and boarded the oncoming train.

I hate surprises and I hate games that involve guessing; it's the powerlessness of it all that turns me off. So when a clown in a subway proves he knows me but won't tell me how or why, I get manic. I ran out of the station and splurged on a cab back to my apartment so Mr. Clown could be immediately Googled. I tried a few advanced search combinations of "Mister" versus "Mr.," which led me to a list of actor bios in a quintuple–Off Broadway production entitled *A Forest Made of Dreams,* which in turn led me to the name Daniel Stewart.

I just about fell off my chair when I read that name.

Daniel Stewart was my boyfriend for a month in 1998, the summer after my freshman year of college when I stayed in New York and worked as an usher at the Lucille Lortel Theater in the West Village. He worked there, too—we worked adjacent aisles—and within a week of meeting, we'd begun spending much of our free time together in his mother's Park Slope brownstone, either watching TV or engaged in rounds of oral sex. After a month I went home to Chicago for the remainder of the summer and we lost touch. Working together six days a week, we'd never gotten around to actually exchanging numbers, and it seemed we'd been lost to each other for good. In the six years that followed, I'd remember him fondly: When you date someone just for a month and keep it simple with reruns of *Three's Company* and the aforementioned oral sex, when all that tears you apart is circumstance, it's easy to keep the gent up on a pedestal. That's where Daniel Stewart was for me, the individual conveniently referred to when other relationships went awry, when I got asked to pee by an acting student or dissed by a hand model. That's when I'd think, *You know who I clicked with? Daniel Stewart. He was fun. One day we'll meet again, I bet, in a cozy coffee shop or wine bar, and give it a second go. Unmarred by my traveling schedule or his mother in the adjacent bedroom scatting along to Cab Calloway albums, our romance will take flight!*

Great reunions like this take time, and I had prepared to wait. I just hadn't prepared for the clown costume or the foam nose and rainbow wig obscuring his identity. Nor had I prepared to see said rainbow wig featured in his online headshot.

Perusing the website for *A Forest Made of Dreams* I realized the show was still playing and I debated whether or not I ought to go to see it. The moment felt very Choose Your Own Adventure:

YOU REALIZE YOUR FORMER FLAME HAS GONE CRAZY!
DO YOU:
A. KEEP THE PAST IN THE PAST AND SPEND FRIDAY NIGHT
ON THE COUCH NURSING YOUR SOUP IN A CUP?!
OR
B. DOUSE YOUR FACE IN TINTED MOISTURIZER,
THEN HIT THE TOWN RUNNING IN YOUR
BEST ATTEMPT TO TRACK HIM DOWN?!

I chose B. After our conversation in the subway, it wasn't so much that I cared to try to reignite the romance, it's more that I felt desperate to know what had happened. How did Daniel Stewart become Mr. Clown? When was the breaking point? What prompted it? Which medications were tried? Did drug use play a part? Also, could I change him back? If yes, fantastic, and so could begin part two of our epic romance. If not, well, that would be less fantastic but at least I'd have some answers to my questions. I knew it would be bold just randomly showing up at his show, but the thing about a man devoted to his clown persona is that it makes him seem all at once vaguely dangerous by virtue of his apparent unhinged-ness but also less intimidating. (While you can fear a clown, you're not necessarily worried what he thinks about you.) So I packed a bottle of No-Doz and a can of mace—to keep me awake during the show and to protect me once it finished—and ventured to this basement theater space on Manhattan's Lower East Side.

A Forest Made of Dreams featured Mr. Clown in the role of Hans Morganstern, a lumberjack who aspires to a future made of something more than chopping wood. The text was written entirely in verse, an ABAB rhyme scheme that included phrases like:

> *There's so much more than this to see!*
> *So much pain in the 'hood!*
> *What is wanted from me?*
> *I'll go chop some more wood!*

It lasted a merciless two and a half hours, and at the end of it I waited for Daniel—or was I supposed to call him Mr. Clown?—outside the front door of the theater. It would've been impossible to play my presence off as a random coincidence, so free as I was from worry about his judgments or looking like a stalker, I explained myself honestly.

"So! Hello again!" I said. "I have to admit, I Googled you after our run-in the other day, just because I was like, 'Ahh! Who *is* that guy?' And anyway, well, I guess I figured it out . . . Daniel." His face twitched when I said "Daniel." "Can I call you Daniel?"

"You can call me whatever you want," he answered, "but understand that now I'm Mr. Clown."

The "now I'm Mr. Clown" seemed promising in comparison to the more adamant "I *am* Mr. Clown," and this encouraged me to keep the conversation going. I asked if he had any plans and, if not, might he like to go and get a beer. "I'd love to catch up," I said, "and hear what you've been up to. Since, you know, it seems like you've got . . . a lot . . . going on."

He told me he refused to frequent bars, and when I asked him why he explained, "Because people in bars always laugh at me."

I pointed out that he was dressed like a clown.

"My intention is to be laughed *with,* never *at,*" he went on. "A clown—*this* clown—should not be a joke, but rather a source of inspiration."

"For *what*?" I asked. And then, fearing I'd sounded counterproductively hostile, I said, "Well, what I mean to say is, what are you hoping to inspire?"

"The gifts of hope and love and laughter."

I'm adept at one-upping people's craziness. Talk to me about the gifts of hope and love inherent in your clowning, and I'll happily outdo you with some anecdote regarding the imaginary friends I had when I was six, the ones I'd talk to only when I moved my bowels. In this conversation, however, I decided I'd let Daniel wear the crazy crown, focused as I was on working out the how and why of his persona. Also, I enjoyed feeling like the normal one for once. I nodded like a gal considering a valid point. "Wow," I said. "What an interesting perspective."

Mr. Clown suggested that instead of a beer in a bar, we go for a walk. "It *would* be nice to catch up," he admitted. "And being outdoors feels safer to me."

To him, sure. But what about the girl on the quasi-date with the full-time clown? It *was* Friday night on the Lower East Side, however, and the streets were packed with hordes of revelers and vomiters and cops and homeless folks, and all this commotion made me feel safe too, I guess, like maybe I wasn't on the verge of a payback for all the date-rape jokes I'd ever made.

Mr. Clown and I began our walk up toward Alphabet City. I asked questions while we walked, and he gave long, circuitous answers that never circled back to asking me what I was up to.

SARA BARRON

This was just as well seeing as how my work in retail sales wasn't something I ever felt compelled to talk about. I learned Daniel Stewart had "disappeared" in 1999, not long after we'd last seen each other. After finishing college upstate, he returned to his mother's brownstone, at which point he was overtaken with an all-encompassing malaise: What should he do with his life? Who was he *really*? Was this all there was? What could he do to make a difference? To really *be* somebody? Then one day he took his five-year-old niece to see the Barnum & Bailey Circus at his mother's urging. Watching all the clowns skip happily around in oversized pajama pants, squirting each other with water-rigged daisies, he realized "clowning was the key to joy." He enrolled in a clown college in San Francisco and emerged two years later as Mr. Clown.

"Why 'Mr. Clown'?" I asked.

"Because I am a man," he answered. "*And* I am a clown."

He never broke from this persona, removing the foam nose only to shower and sleep, responding only to the title Mr. Clown, exhibiting a long-term level of commitment with a graceful bit of tattooed calligraphy sprawled across his lower back that said, THE CLOWN IS LOVE. I know that's what it said because he showed me.

"I owe the clown my life," he said. "And so I *give* the clown my life."

Whether thanks to Stephen King's *It* or John Wayne Gacy's face paint, I know a lot of people fear clowns, but I've always kept my associations less complex and menacing. I think first of balloon animals and oversized lips. I was poised to find Mr. Clown's company delightful or at least amusing, but the more we walked and talked, I just got to feeling depressed. "Clown" meant joy and laughter to Daniel Stewart, but now to me, it just meant slaughtered hopes for romance and a blatant manifestation of my own insensitive and exploitative tendencies. Daniel had gone a form of crazy that seemed to surpass entertaining and land on tragic, and here I was motivated by wanting sex or romance, or at least a laugh at his expense. The disappointment and self-loathing got me feeling short of breath, which made me crave a shot of amaretto. Well, there'd be no amaretto at a bar with Mr. Clown, which was how and when and why I figured it was time for us to go our separate ways.

When we reached Union Square, the sight of our reunion, I braced for an awkward good-bye. I imagined a 24/7 clown didn't log much time with the ladies, and by simple virtue of not having shied away from his persona, I automatically presumed I'd be asked out for another walk or approached for a kiss. I was preparing a sensitive rejection when he suggested we kill some time on a nearby park bench. "My girlfriend's on her way, but she won't be here for a bit," he said. "Wanna sit and wait?"

For seventy-two hours I'd been consumed by the question "What happened to Daniel Stewart?" Well, that flipped in an instant to "Who *dates* Daniel Stewart?" I expected a bearded lady or one-armed ventriloquist, but five minutes later a shockingly beautiful Bolivian woman arrived. In timid, accented English she muttered, "Oh. Hall-oooo," while grabbing Daniel's hand. She was normal by all outward appearances, and she cuddled against him as he encouraged me to come to the back car of the R train some weekday afternoon to check out his juggling show, a performance he described as much more "me" than *A Forest Made of Dreams*.

I said I would but knew I wouldn't and watched as he put his arm around his girlfriend and escorted her away.

As the clown and the Bolivian got smaller in the distance, I wondered who my other half might be. Daniel Stewart had been the default face on this otherwise ambiguous fantasy for years; what vision should replace him? If the standards in New York are such that a clown gets an ESL-ed stunner, what was I to hope for? I figured it best to keep my options open and scanned the streets for any man without a wig.

the janitor

I would sooner spoon a clown or hump a dwarf than I would a man who wears cologne. I *hate* cologne. It turns my stomach faster than hair plugs or a poor endowment, and the real tragedy of working at Banana Republic was that every man I came across smelled like he'd smeared the stuff from head to sac. As a result, I endured a long, rough patch of celibacy. In my darkest, most frustrated hours I'd think, *I might just have to buckle. If I want to have sex ever again, I might just have to do it with a man who wears cologne.*

There was an employee bathroom at Banana Republic, and awkwardly constructed as it was out of plywood and beige tiles, it begged for graffiti. One afternoon, I went for a midshift pee and saw scrawled on the bathroom door, I WANT CHOCOLATE SARA B!

I wondered what it meant. Did someone want chocolate *from* me? Was it a reference to me being sweet? An invitation for a Dirty Sanchez? I couldn't be too sure. Then the next day another scrawl appeared in the same handwriting that said, TE AMO SARA. USTED

UN BUENO CULO. And the day after that, yet another one appeared, this an illustration of my ass with a penis ejaculating onto it. I used deductive reasoning to determine that the anonymous artist was:

1. of the Central or South American persuasion

2. interested in having sex with me

3. a coworker and therefore a cologne enthusiast.

Normally #3 would be a deal breaker, but I hadn't had sex in six months, and so #2 was enough to get me interested. I searched for clues. I asked my coworkers, "Does anyone know who drew the picture of my ass and the penis in the employee bathroom?"

"I *saw* that!" said Mike. "That's blatant sexual harassment! You should complain to management, you really should."

"Why?" I asked. "I'm not angry."

"No?" he asked.

"No," I said. "Not at all. I haven't had sex in six months."

"How is that related?"

"Well, frankly, I feel like I shouldn't waste an opportunity."

Mike gasped then and started massaging his forehead as if to smooth out a headache. "Are you trying to tell me that you plan to chase a man just because he wrote 'nice ass' in Sharpie on plywood?"

I gave a grimace of acknowledgement as if to say, *Is that* that *outlandish?*

"Jesus. Well, all right. If you're serious, then I'm pretty sure that Jorge did it."

"Jorge!" I screamed. "Of *course*!" I clapped my hands together as Mike scribbled something on a scrap of paper. "What's that? His number? Why do *you* have Jorge's number?"

"I don't," he said. "That's my therapist, Sheila Epstein. I want you to give her a call."

I ignored the condescending offer and refocused on my newest prospect. Jorge was a nineteen-year-old Ecuadorian with a lush, black pompadour and a carrot-shaped constellation of moles on

155

his right cheek. He'd been hired as the on-site janitor at Banana Republic a month earlier and though we'd never been formally introduced, I had caught him eyeing me on occasion, then miming a humping motion once he'd done so. I hadn't found him previously attractive, but the more I got to thinking about it, the more I felt bombarded by his winning aspects: He didn't wear cologne and, in the sea of aforementioned khaki, opted for low-slung baggy jeans. Also, it sounded like fun to let what I hoped would be our knack for gangbuster amour-making bridge the language gap between us.

Several days later we found ourselves alone in the stockroom. "*Hola*, Jorge," I said. "*Cómo estás?*"

Men who flirt by drawing a picture of their penis ejaculating onto you aren't usually shy, and Jorge was no exception. All I did was establish eye contact and offer up a generic pleasantry and he was on me, having pinned my back against a shelf of back-stocked wool slacks. He started thrusting violently against me like some sort of dog or motorized man doll. The exchange was unpleasant: The wool slacks itched against my neck, and what was worse was that Jorge wore his cell phone on his belt and it kept cracking again and again against my pubic bone. A cell phone on a belt always makes me uncomfortable emotionally, and this addition of the physical discomfort made the circumstance downright intolerable.

"Jorge!" I said, and spattered saliva on his face, covered as I was thanks to his flurry of leech-y kisses (he'd attach, then suck). "Stop!" He ignored me. I repeated. "Stop! Jorge! Stop!"

Forget the reunion with the questionably dangerous, oddball clown, I thought; *here* was my due for all my date-rape jokes. Would this be the end? Would I ever get him off me? An *Oprah* episode came to mind in which she had discussed what women ought to do if physically attacked. For one, you're not supposed to leave the original spot of the attack, and for another, you're supposed to act like *you're* the crazy one. If you can get yourself to shit or vomit, do so. Pretend to hear voices. Feign schizophrenia. That course of action seemed a tad on the dramatic side for my Jorge encounter, however, so I did a quick mental calculation of what *would* be appropriate. *Feign IBS!* I thought.

"Jorge," I repeated, and pointed at my FUPA. "Me. *Baño. Ahora.*"

I didn't meet my end in that Banana Republic stockroom or anything close to it. Jorge's domineering ways stopped as quickly as they started with a deft and well-timed motion toward my small intestine. And one week later, just as I found myself stuck in this exhausting back-and-forth about whether or not I ought to report him to the higher-ups—had I not asked for what I'd gotten? Was there truth to the rumor that he saved the money he earned at Banana Republic to send it home to his mother in Ecuador? Was a heavy dose of sexual harassment enough to want to cramp such noble plans?—he was fired for stealing a leather jacket out of the very same stockroom where our pelvis jam occurred. Still, I felt like I'd flirted with an unwise amount of danger and wondered if Mike had been more on target than I'd originally admitted in suggesting I call Sheila Epstein.

Therapists like to open a first session with the question, "So tell me why you're here," and this one was no different. Five days later I had an appointment and gave Sheila Epstein the boiled-down version: "Well, my friend gave me your number after a guy at work wrote degrading stuff about me on the walls in the employee bathroom and instead of making me angry, it made me want to sleep with him because—well, ay! There's the rub, isn't it? Well. Anyway."

Sheila Epstein nodded and told me what I'd said was interesting, then asked if the behavioral pattern I'd just mapped out was one I'd ever exhibited before. I rattled off something about clowns and homosexuals, then watched the minutes on the faux-vintage Pottery Barn clock tick by. Sheila Epstein was similar to my childhood therapist Barbara Levy in that she knocked out a series of leading questions. The difference was, Sheila's were less specific and therefore—impossibly—even more annoying. After my initial admission and her follow-up question about patterns, all she'd say in response was "And?" or "Why?" or "Why do you think that is?"

It was unexpectedly excruciating. I always thought I'd take well to the therapeutic arts since the lingo was familiar from my mom *and* I'm good at focusing on myself. But over the course of several sessions with Sheila Epstein, I found the amount of required introspection exhausting. It's no walk in the park to delve into issues of self-loathing, self-worth, and self-indulgence when what you're after is a quick fix.

"Hey, Sheila," I interrupted toward the end of our fourth session. She'd branched out question-wise with something as specific as "Do you think that's rooted in your mother's anger?" But I had other things I cared to talk about. "I know that everything you've said is valid," I began, "but I feel like this is *years'* worth of baggage we're looking at, and frankly my budget can't afford that." While confrontational, this was also direct. And though she'd encouraged me to worry less about what other people thought, I hoped that such directness would appease her.

Sheila responded with something about "priorities" and "sliding scales." She tempted me with promises of "building" my "self-confidence" so I'd learn to "feel entitled" to "have standards."

"That sounds great," I said, "really great. But the thing is, I'm not meeting anyone worth having standards for."

"That's just a self-fulfilling prophecy."

"I'm not so sure about that. I think it's the result of working at Banana Republic and being surrounded exclusively by men who wear cologne. What I need is a better sense of options." Sheila Epstein rambled on about how being complete within oneself was the healthy groundwork from which to begin looking for a mate. "That *also* sounds great," I interrupted again, "and if I get a raise sometime soon, I'd love to talk more about that. But what can I do to find someone *now*? Even if I'm not going about it in the most productive way. Any pointers? Please? Honestly, I feel like I'm staring down a lifetime's worth of solitude."

"You're not," said Sheila Epstein with a sigh. "What you *are* doing is called 'playing victim,' but we can talk about that later. In the meantime, have you thought about a singles' mixer? Or online dating?"

The phrase *singles' mixer* kicked my IBS into gear *for real,* so that was out. But online dating sounded reasonable enough: anonymous until it didn't have to be, until I'd decided of my own volition to accept a date with (let's just say for the sake of example) the attractive and successful Broadway producer whom I wouldn't otherwise have had the chance to meet.

"Online dating," I repeated. "That *does* sound good."

Sheila nodded benevolently. "I'm glad you think so. But do keep in mind that I still have appointments available next week if you decide you'd like to come in. My sense is that you'd benefit from delving further into this fundamental fear of solitude. I think it's contributing to your feelings of inadequacy."

Does that sound like fun? Paying good money to delve into feelings of inadequacy? No. No, it does not. Sheila Epstein cost $80 a pop and for that same amount of money, I could have three whole months' worth of unlimited access to men of all colors, shapes, styles, and professions! It's like they say in commercials where they compare one thing that's supposed to be obviously awful (introspection) to something else that's supposed to be obviously not (*mas* hombres!): The choice was clear.

love at first site

Some people feel ashamed or embarrassed at turning to the Internet for help in their love life. Not me. Get molested by a janitor, and you get over that. What I was having trouble with was deciding which site to use. There were so many options available and everyone suggested something different: my mom suggested JDate for the Jews; Maggie suggested Match.com because she'd heard the guys there were less likely to have STDs. *Less likely than whom?* I wondered, though never asked, writing the trivia off as another questionable piece of her incessant disease-related Googling. Mike suggested Nerve.com because that's where he'd met his latest boyfriend, Ronnie. I considered the options. JDate was out because I had zero interest in dating someone who'd date me only on the condition of my Jew-ness. I'd been down that road before (*see:* Randall Buckwald and other, less noteworthy dalliances with men named Max or Ben or Noah) and every time—after having been paraded around at some Bat or Bar Mitzvah—these guys would ask me to dress up like a Catholic schoolgirl. Every time. It always happened behind closed doors and always around month four or five of the relationship. In the throes of one particularly dramatic role-play scenario, one particular Benjamin went the extra mile of asking if he could call me "Tina."

"Tina?" I'd asked. "As in "CHRIST-ina?! As in the name more steeped in gentile than any other in the world?!"

I blamed not the dalliers for these antics, but rather the parents of the dalliers. They were the ones who'd put us Jewish gals up on the pedestal of proper dating and in so doing shoved the blond-haired, cross-wearing gentiles squarely into the seductive corner. Now some Shiksa McGee got to play Forbidden Fruit while *I* had to field requests for a blond wig or plaid skirt. (*Oy vey*, I thought. *No, gracias.* Or, you know, however it is you say "no, thank you" in Yiddish.) And Match.com—despite Maggie's endorsement—was also out once I took stock of the pickings: The first three profiles I stumbled across were of men named SexyLikeULikeIt, ProudPapaof2, and BeautyAndTruth. All these gents were in their late forties seeking women in their mid-twenties, and they all sported the Caesar hairstyle of George Clooney circa 1993. Perhaps I should've been more patient and investigated the wealth of Match.com options more thoroughly, but a gal's told threefold her romantic options are daddy-ish figures with a sense of entitlement gone wilder than a coed in Cancun, and frankly, she feels drained of such patience. So I decided on Nerve.com. I was seduced by the fact that the first few profiles I came across showcased young men in medical school wearing cool glasses, and I decided that one of them, LuckyJim_28, was meant to be my soul mate. He had nicely groomed facial hair and wore my favorite kind of glasses, which is the thick-framed, black kind that evoke Woody Allen circa *Annie Hall:* pre-pedophilia, pre–*The Curse of the Jade Scorpion*. In the list of items he said he couldn't live without, LuckyJim listed his Martha Stewart pie-crust mold (for baking, he specified), and also a gun for killing every MySpace "friend" who'd ever had the balls to question why they'd been dropped from his "Top 8." I found these answers funny and endearing, but topping them both was his response to the question "What's Your Favorite On-Screen Sex Scene?" LuckyJim wrote, "Kyle MacLachlan and Elizabeth Berkley in *Showgirls* enjoying a champagne toast before hopping (and humping!) in the Olympic-size swimming pool . . . It gets me every time."

Showgirls is my favorite movie ever made. While I've been told other people experience a feeling of contented wholeness when they hear a child laugh or watch the sunset with a loved one, I reserve that sensation for the experience of watching Elizabeth Berkley's Nomi Malone learn choreography as she dances and schemes her way to the top. And while other people won't date outside their religious group (*see:* JDate) or political party, I can't be with a man who fails to see the comedic genius manifest in this Berkley pièce de résistance. I wanted LuckyJim_28 to know that no other woman would love Berkley more or MySpace less, so I registered at Nerve.com so I could tell him so.

The first order of business was creating a username and "headline." Before committing to any one choice, however, I thought it might be wise to browse the site and see what other women had come up with. I learned that, generally speaking, they fell into four categories: romantic, strong-willed, suggestive, or straightforward. The romantic ladies had usernames like Water_and_Roses or Sweet_in_the_City. They all liked museums, confessed to holding on to their childhood "blankie," and more often than not, the sentence "I really DO love long walks on the beach!" could be found in their "About Me" sections. Conversely, the strong-willed types wanted to convey their "fierce," "passionate" nature and so chose usernames like "FuelForYourFire" or "Adventure_Seeker." They wanted "partners in crime" yet were unwilling to sacrifice their "independent nature," and *their* headlines went something like, "If you think you can handle it . . ." or "If you're the type that likes a challenge . . ."

The suggestive ones had the habit of combining an erotic adjective with their given borough of residence, e.g. "Bothered_in_Brooklyn" or "SillySexyManhattan," and their photos featured them in one of two fabrics: velvet or leopard print. One woman showcased herself in leopard-print velvet, went by the username "Lovin'_Life _in_NYC," and answered the "More of What I'm Looking For" question with: "A man who'll hold me . . . and HOLD! ME! DOWN!"

Rounding out these groups were the straightforward, seemingly more multidimensional women. I wanted to try to join their ranks, and so as my username I chose the uncreative but appropriate "sara_b" and as my headline, "Well THIS is awkward." Because, well, it was. I downloaded a photo of myself in a polka-dot dress and e-mailed LuckyJim_28 the following: "If nothing else, my day has gotten brighter knowing there's another person on the planet who appreciates Elizabeth Berkley's otherwise underappreciated gift for comedy." His reply—"Well hello sara_b. Glad to meet a kindred spirit"—came later that same night. I liked the brevity of both the e-mail and the response time—neither overly eager nor too hard-to-get—and after a few more back-and-forths, we set up a date at an East Village bar.

It was only once LuckyJim arrived (ten minutes late and jabbering apologies) that I realized he was a midget.

Whether it was a case of clinical dwarfism or not, I didn't know. All that registered was his hairline: It had receded significantly since the time of his profile photo and stood flush with my elbows. I thought to myself, *Well, at least we'll be sitting down,* but as it turned out, no. There weren't enough seats at the bar, so LuckyJim—as much a gentleman as he was a *Showgirls* connoisseur—offered me the one available stool and volunteered to stand. I don't recall the specifics of our conversation. All I remember is that I smiled and nodded a lot and snapped to attention only when Jim, having had a few drinks, worked up the nerve (pun intended!) to ask, "So tell me: How come you like little guys?"

I found this question problematic. It suggested that Lucky-Jim_28 had, in fact, addressed his physical stature in his online profile. Which in turn suggested that upon sending him an e-mail, I'd known what I was getting into.

Whenever I find myself in an awkward situation that is someone else's fault, I like to tell them so and milk the guilt for what it's worth: beer, money, physical affection, etc. But if I find myself in a situation in which *I'm* the one to blame, I prefer to shirk responsibility by making an immediate departure. Here, I'd falsely presented myself as some sort of dwarf fetishist, so after an hour I stood up and stretched like, *Oh* boy! *Am* I *tired!* which was when LuckyJim, drunk to the point of slurring after two shots of whiskey, decided to spoon me vertically. He stretched his arms all the way around my waist, rested his head in the small of my back, then let out a deep, contented sigh. He said, "Not a bad fit, am I right?"

Well sure, I thought, *if you want a piggyback.* But judging from how cozy he was getting, and at the risk of a self-aggrandizing assumption, I sensed LuckyJim wanted more than just a piggyback. So I peeled him off me, laid a twenty on the bar, thanked him for the date, and left. I wasn't thrilled with the aggressive and presumptuous vertical spoon, that much was true, but if I'm being really honest, I dashed when I did because he was a midget. This made me feel awful and ashamed. And maybe if I hadn't just spent eighty bucks on my Nerve.com membership, I would've called up Sheila Epstein and talked through some of this burgeoning self-loathing with her. But circumstances being what they were, I headed home instead to dull it with a bottle of amaretto and my Nerve.com inbox. In the three hours I'd been out, I'd received fifteen new e-mails. The first was from HotMatthew, a self-described "New Jersey–based liberal broadcasting executive and model." I was told by HotMatthew that if he looked familiar it was because I'd seen him in various publications, including *Men's Health* and the Ralph Lauren fall catalog. HotMatthew was also a spontaneous adventure-seeker. "As I am a spontaneous adventure-seeker," he wrote, "I would love to have you join me for dinner and drinks! 914-555-2991 is my number. Make the call!

Don't be shy! Cya soon I hope. —Matthew." I didn't plan to make the call and shyness wasn't why. An abbreviation like "cya"—that, and also "LOL" and "lemino" and "ya" and emoticons and the word "cheers" as a send-off from someone who's not British—all these devices wiggled into texts or e-mails, they set me ill at ease. And while I suppose I wouldn't much have minded dating a model, I didn't think I'd fare that well with someone *proud* to be a model. I deleted the e-mail.

The next one came from Father_of_a_Harvard_Grad, a fifty-five-year-old with a visibly distended stomach who wrote only: "My wife's away . . . Do you think sara_b would like to play?" This was the first in a series of sexually suggestive queries I'd receive. A young man in Trenton wrote, "You lookin' sexy 'n thick, gurl. You got the body 4 the brothas to cum after," and from Seek_it!Find_it!Love_it!, a "confident, rugged young film-maker": "Think you can handle THIS?" Then I scrolled down to find a nude photo of the rugged filmmaker in the lotus position with his hands wrapped around his genitals. Next came another e-mail from Father_of_a_Harvard_Grad, this one composed around a rhyme scheme. It read, "S.B. is kinky . . . She wanna go get a drinky?" and from a suitor named The_Wiley_Dutchman: "Wanna fuck and chuck?"

What's "chuck"? I thought.

The_Wiley_Dutchman answered my question in a follow-up e-mail:

> *Hi. My name's Andre. I wrote that other e-mail to you last night when I was drunk. I don't know if it made sense or any-thing, but what I meant was that I'm interested in a sex part-ner ONLY, so I'd like to fuck if you would, and then we'd chuck each other when we're done.*

The_Wiley_Dutchman looked to be about six feet tall and—judging from his profile photo, which featured him hoisting a bar-bell above his head—a professional weight lifter. I decided if the

fucking didn't kill me, the chucking probably would. I deleted the
e-mail.

The next—and the first with a hint of promise—came from
a twenty-eight-year-old Asian man who went by the username
Let's_Explore_2gether. Like The_Wiley_Dutchman, Let's_Explore_
2gether wrote a thorough explanation of his situation:

> Hi Sara_b. I like your polka-dot dress. You wear it well. Any-
> way, I'll get to the point: I recently ended a pretty much sex-
> less three-year relationship. Please help me! I want to explore
> things sexually and I want to explore them with you! You are
> breathtaking! Do you have MSN Messenger or Yahoo! Mes-
> senger? Take care, Tang.

I liked the fact that Tang had taken the time to compliment my
dress and refer to me as "breathtaking," and I liked that he was
Asian. I hadn't dated an Asian guy at that point and after you
read enough online profiles wherein people describe themselves as
"adventurous" or "adventure seekers," you can't help but think
that maybe you too could stand for a little horizon broadening. I
thought to myself, *What am I waiting for if not a guy who knows
a well-fitting dress when he sees one?* and forwarded the e-mail to
Maggie. I wanted a second opinion. At the top I wrote, "What do
you think? Could be interesting, no?"

Maggie wrote back, "Let's_Explore_2gether just spelled out
'Date Rape' in sixty words or less. Twenty bucks says LuckyJim's
profile said 'I AM A MIDGET' in bold letters across the top and
you missed it because you have no reading comprehension skills."

A fair point, I had to admit. I deleted the e-mail.

The next one came from a gentleman whose username was
Poetry_dogg. "Divinity is in the face of an angel," he wrote, "and
you are that angel. I can tell that you are what I seek: someone
who understands the demands of an artist, who enjoys the
moments of inspiration and the hours of passion. I am looking
for my sonnet . . . my angel."

Poetry_dogg's e-mail was lengthy and went on to explain a bit more about himself: "I am no one and nothing, everything and something. I am the puzzle of pieces, a metronome of sound, a creator of passion, a man and a clown. I am proudly stating the fact, the recipe and the desire. I am what you were warned about, dreamed of and longed for. I am."

I've been warned about moles that change shape and under-cooked beef, but at no point has someone told me, "Beware the metronome of sound." Poetry_dogg, while likely not the human fulfillment of *my* hopes and dreams, still came across as a barrel of laughs. And considering how blue I felt about the Lucky Jim deba-cle, I was in no position to let an opportunity for laughter slip by. I e-mailed back to set up a date. We could share a few beers, I thought, and discuss what my role as sonnet/angel might entail.

I knew that in order to keep Poetry_dogg's interest, I'd have to speak his language. I wrote back, "A million thank yous for a beautiful e-mail. You possess something soulful and amazing. Let us meet . . . the sooner the better."

In his response, Poetry_dogg suggested an Upper East Side tea-house and I agreed. We met the following afternoon. The Dogg arrived in a Chinese silk pajama top carrying a red rose. "A red rose is a gift for an angel," he told me. "Now read the card." Written in cursive on the outside of the envelope were the words "Love Is a Many-Splendored Thing," and then inside the card was a poem titled "In the Eye of the Beholder Is All the Love We Need." "In the eye of the beholder is all the love we need," it began, and continued:

to see us through this journey / our journey / Called life / I have looked and looked for love / And wholeness / Have I found you? / Will I find you? / You will be in the face of an angel, this much I know / Take my hand and we go forth / like pilgrims / like lovers / like all that is true.

Poetry_dogg interrupted my reading to ask if anyone had ever written a poem for me before.

"This one guy wrote out the lyrics to the Seal song 'Kiss from a Rose' on a doily for me once," I said. This tidbit is both true and, I think, hilarious, and so I hoped Poetry_dogg would enjoy it. But it seemed rather to annoy him. When I'd said the phrase "Seal song" he let out an exasperated sigh like he thought I was an idiot. *He* was in a silk pajama top but *I* was the idiot because *I'd* failed to distinguish between "I've been kissed by a rose on the sea" and the decidedly more sophisticated "In the Eye of the Beholder Is All the Love We Need." Well, if he was going to sit and pout, that was fine by me. I excel at filling awkward silence with mindless chatter. I said, "I liked the 'Kiss from a Rose' song as much as the next person, but at a certain point it's like, '*Why* must Seal insist on wearing suits without a shirt underneath, you know? I mean, does he think that looks good? Is it something his publicist told him to do?" I rambled on until Poetry_dogg lifted his head from his hands. I thought he was going to say something like "What a good point!" or "I've been saying that for years!" but instead he just stared at a table of women seated across from us, all of them clad in Lycra pants and Juicy Couture hoodies, all of them holding a yoga mat. He stared at them desirously. He stared at them like he was thinking, *I bet one of* those *girls would make a better sonnet/angel*.

The vaguest hint I'm being rejected for someone more adept at doing downward dog and I'm suddenly capable of turning a blind eye to red roses and silk pajama tops. To get me interested, I don't need love; I need rejection. Ideally, I take it with a dash of jealousy thrown in for good measure and the way I saw it, this metronome of sound had just served up the perfect helping over tea. The moment I sensed he thought me underqualified to be his sonnet/angel, choruses of *Maybe he's not so bad* echoed in rounds in my mind. After all, I thought, the Dogg *was* a "creator of passions," albeit one who created said passions with a long-stemmed rose and a half-cup of Drakkar Noir. And he *was* a self-described "puzzle of pieces." Maybe that meant he'd be complex, unpredictable, and full of surprises. Maybe it meant he'd be mysterious.

I'd heard a lot of people say that mystery is the key to a successful relationship. Maria Shriver said so once on *Oprah* in describing her marriage to Arnold Schwarzenegger. She said it worked as well as it did because there was still some mystery between them, because Arnold was the kind of man who always kept her guessing.

I bet the Dogg could keep me *guessing,* I thought. I could guess things like, "What'll he write about today?" or "If pajamas are for daytime, what does he have to wear at night?"

I backpedaled to try to regain favor. "You wanna know what?" I asked. "I loved that line 'we go forth like pilgrims.' That was . . . wow. It really took me . . . on a journey."

"I wrote that line from a very dark place," said the Dogg.

"I sensed that," I responded, "seeing as how the poem feels so . . . charged."

After I said the word *charged,* Poetry_dogg looked at me adoringly and reached for my hand. Then he turned it over and started tracing something on my palm.

"Do you know what I'm doing?" he asked.

"Are you writing a poem?" I asked back. "In my hand?"

He told me he was, and that the poem was titled "A Queen for the Millennium." "Queen for the Millennium," he recited. "Oh queen / Oh queen / Let me see myself reflected in your smile / Now / Let me see you / Let me really see you smile."

I don't like smiling under regular circumstances because I think it makes my cheeks look fat. Add to that baseboard of dislike an unironic poetry recitation entitled "Queen for the Millennium" and the event becomes as likely as the Dogg's poems getting published. I deflected the request by saying, "Let me see *you* smile." I was the queen after all, and so he did as I requested. That's when I noticed his oddly swollen gums. Now, I must point out that my mom has always told me to be wary of men with poor dental hygiene. "Steer clear," she warns, "it means they're irresponsible." And suddenly it dawned on me! *This* was what he'd meant by "I am what you were warned about . . ."

I had to accept that it would never work between the Dogg and me. While the poems would keep coming, a group of Lycra-clad women on hand to keep him distracted and me interested seemed an unsafe bet. So I took his hand in mine and said, "You are so much. Of so many things"—and here I stood up from the table—"that I almost forgot . . . my hair appointment." And then I grabbed my jacket off the back of the chair and inched toward the door, prepared for him to say "Parting is such sweet sorrow." Which he did.

The next day I received three new messages in my Nerve.com inbox. Two of the three came from the same person, a German investment banker named Show_Me_the_Money in an obvious toupee. The first read:

> *Greetings pretty one! Your dress bangs! I'm actually writing this note to the dress! Note to the dress: you are SO awesome. Also: Note to the woman in the dress: Why are YOU looking for people online? Is it that you've met awful people where you live? I'm interested. Anyhoo, tell me this: What's your favorite planet?*

Before responding, "Is there anyone out there who *wouldn't* say 'Uranus'?" I figured I ought to peruse his second e-mail. It said:

> *I should not have sent you that message when I came home last night. I was drunk and I think I was carried away by your dress. But I just re-read your profile and I'm not actually that interested in you. You seem okay I guess, but not enough of what I'm looking for to really hold my interest. Thanks anyway.*

I thought Show_Me_the_Money deserved a response. I wrote back:

> *Greetings Show_Me_the_Money! I know you have on a toupee! Your toupee bangs! I'm actually writing this note to*

*the toupee! Note to the toupee: You are obvious! Also: Note
to the man in the toupee: Have you been snorting crack?*

Then I attached a link to a hair-transplant website.

The third e-mail came from Get_Awesome, a twenty-seven-year-old photographer in Brooklyn. The name "Get_Awesome" didn't bode well as I thought it evoked someone pining away for his college days. I imagined him at any one of a number of frat parties screaming, "GET DRUNK! GET LAID! GET AWESOME!" before attaching himself to a beer bong or the breasts of a girl blacked out on the floor. The invented scenario didn't thrill me, but what did were the facts that Get_Awesome had sent an intentionally funny e-mail and that his profile photo revealed the biggest hands I'd ever seen. The e-mail read:

> *Hey Sara_b. A couple of things: 1) I appreciate any woman
> who owns up to having memorized the first and last names
> of all the members of 'N Sync, and 2) If you agree to get a
> beer with me, I promise not to play the air guitar [In my
> "About You" I'd written: "You do not play air instruments of
> any kind."] although I promise nothing about the air French
> horn if I've had a French martini . . . which is a girl drink I
> realize, but I still love them. —George.*

George seemed like the kind of guy I could really get along with. I forwarded the e-mail to Maggie, who wrote back, "Go out with him! Get_Awesome has the biggest hands I've ever seen!"

In person, George's hands looked big enough to crack a skull. I stared at them incessantly as we chatted about his taste for sweet cocktails and why "God Must Have Spent a Little More Time on You" is my favorite song off 'N Sync's first album. Three hours and ten beers later, we'd both loosened up enough to grope good night. We stood on a street corner and enjoyed the balmy autumn evening, the whole thing feeling very romantic until a homeless man yelled, "YOU GOTTA TAP THAT WHILE SHE'S DRUNK!"

George refrained, however, and I remained untapped that night. Not only did I remain untapped *that* night, I remained untapped over the course of the two-month relationship we carried on afterward. After our first few dates, I learned that Get_Awesome was that rare breed of gent who liked to take things slow. Fine. So we did a lot of talking. We talked about Get_Awesome's Xanax addiction, his germ phobia, his weekly visits to the New York Clinic for Obsessive-Compulsive Disorders. It wasn't until our seventh date that he admitted, "I won't have sex with a woman unless I've put on three condoms."

"Three?" I asked. "Really? Can you feel anything that way?"

"Not really," he confirmed. "But have you ever heard of 'stuffing'?"

Years ago, I was listening to some radio sex show when a woman called wanting to know what to do with her husband, who couldn't get an erection anymore. As a solution, the radio host suggested "stuffing." "The man stuffs his flaccid penis into the woman's vagina," the talk-show host explained, "and leaves it there. And while this might not bring the woman to her climax, the action *can* generate sensual feelings of arousal."

So I told George I *had* heard of "stuffing." "And while I love it in a turkey," I went on, "I love it less between my legs."

Well that was that. Game over. Done. You get to talking flaccidity with a man under thirty and exhibit anything less than a worshipful show of support once he's come clean—"That's fine! *Totally* fine!"—and he'll dump you faster than a spicy curry dinner.

One week later I was back on the Nerve.com circuit, enjoying a beer with Let_Love_Live, a former Peace Corps member who was now working in real estate. During our first round of drinks he asked, "You're thinking, *After the Peace Corps, why real estate? Right?*" What I'd actually been thinking was, *I wish your hands had been visible in your profile photo so I would've known ahead of time you wear a pinky ring.* Instead I just nodded and said, "Right. Yes. What an interesting career path. Please explain further."

"Well, let me just tell you. I've taught enough children in enough countries to let *my* soul rest easy for a while. Have *you* ever single-handedly lifted an African child from the jaws of poverty?"

"No," I said. "Have you? With a hand that sports a pinky ring?"

Over the course of the next month I received a series of other e-mails from individuals like Which_Way_to_Heaven, a forty-two-year-old wine distributor looking for "that nicefunsexy-smartgirl who knows which way the wind blows, so she can whisper the answer in my ear"; Substance_and_Sass, a twenty-three-year-old law student who wrote, "I want to run my fingers down the back of your neck before I wrap my hands around your throat"; and Celebrate_Good_Times!, a Fordham University college student, who e-mailed me a list of DJs who "spin like their shit's on fire!" and wanted to know who among them was my favorite. I sorted through them all and went on two more dates. The first was with Sing_Like_You_Think_No_One's_Listening, a jazz musician who looked good on paper but spent the majority of our date doing improvisational scats, and the second with One_Love_One_Life, who said in his profile that he was really passionate about his work in anthropology. It was only once we spoke in person that I realized he meant the women's clothing store and not the field. Even so, working in retail wasn't the problem. The problem was that he was "really passionate about it!"

One week later Nerve.com sent me an e-mail saying it was time to renew my membership; they were making a special holiday offer and promised I'd get my money back if I didn't meet that "special someone" within the next three months. I clicked the box marked "no." I didn't see the point of continuing the search seeing as how I'd already encountered enough online "special-ness" to last a lifetime. Nerve.com had taught me that an evening home alone spent watching *Oprah* while munching on a cheese wheel was not an event to be so quickly disregarded. And that's a valuable lesson. It's just that having it confirmed wasn't worth another eighty bucks.

orthopedics

excuse me, miss?

When you grow up in a Jewish suburb, you've seen a production of *The Diary of Anne Frank* at least twice by the time you turn eighteen. Maybe three times. Maybe there's a day when with your Hebrew school in tow, you see back-to-back showings of *Anne Frank* AND *Schindler's List*. On that day you remember suffering. On that day you remember the strength and resilience of the Jewish people. Anne Frank had borne witness to some of history's worst atrocities, you learn, and *still* maintained an optimistic view. *Still* she thought of man as being good at heart. It's a sentiment I've always tried to keep in mind. But then one day my life took a dramatic turn: I became a waiter. At the Olive Garden. And suddenly such full-throttle optimism became an unabashed impossibility.

I'd quit Banana Republic so I could tend bar in a half shirt. Once that venture failed, I still worked sporadically as both an actor (I won the role of Woman with Anthrax in a short film Maggie made about her hypochondria) and comedian (once a month I'd serve as the opening act for Ida Slapter's solo show *The Tortoise and the Hair*), but none of it paid the bills. Unqualified for everything, I tried to think in terms of my most basic abilities.

"I'm good at eating," I told myself. "Perhaps I ought to be a waiter."

The idea seemed pleasant enough. Over the course of several weeks, I wandered into different New York dining establishments to see if they were hiring. Most were not. This sort of constant negativity took its toll on my ability to self-motivate, especially since when I finally stumbled upon a place that *was* hiring, the managers would ask me these absurd, disheartening questions, such as, "Have you ever waited tables before?" or "Do you have any experience in the restaurant industry?"

"Not technically, no," became my stock response, "but I *do* have a vivacious personality that I think compensates for my lack of traditional 'experience.'"

It's a stock response I'd say with a twinkle in my eye, a stock response I *thought* might appeal to my potential employers for its sense of humor and forthrightness. But no. All I got in response were raised eyebrows or exhausted sighs, and then I'd be shown the door. After a while, I got the hint: It was time to lower my standards. *Well, then fine,* I'd tell myself, *just think bottom of the barrel. Just think "What environment will best allow my incompetence to blend?"*

There's an Olive Garden in New York City situated on the corner of Forty-seventh Street and Broadway, and I used to walk by it during my dalliance with the hand model, whose apartment was on Forty-ninth. One time I wandered in to use the bathroom, but the hostess, gnawing at a hangnail and reeking terribly of marijuana, couldn't remember where it was. "Um, it's near the back, I think?" she answered. "Oh, wait. No! Sorry, I'm totally out of it. I think, actually, that it's up the stairs and on your right." So adorably unprofessional was she, so wonderfully content in her blatant incompetence, that I decided what I ought to do was see if *her* employer was hiring. I wandered in one weekday afternoon

178

and asked to speak with the Olive Garden manager. A man stuffed tightly into pewter slacks came to my assistance. "May I help you?" he asked. He was sweating profusely.

"I think so," I answered. "I was interested to know if you had any waiter positions open at the moment."

"We do, actually," he said. "Have you ever waited tables before?"

"Not technically, no," I acknowledged, "but I *do* have a vivacious personality that I think compensates for my lack of traditional 'experience.'"

I'd geared up for the eye roll, but this manager surprised me by saying, "Really?! Well, that's awesome! Because here at the Olive Garden, go-getters are exactly what we're looking for! I mean, heck, I can teach you to wait tables, but a great attitude is just something you're born with!"

Saying I have a great attitude is like saying I have a penis. I don't. I mean, perhaps if someone chose to ignore every piece of evidence to the contrary, someone could trick herself into thinking otherwise. Like if I was walking down the street in a parka and a pair of gender-neutral boots, you might not know for sure. I guess my disguise was equally effective when I walked into the Olive Garden and made reference to my "vivacious personality," because after a ten-minute interview, this manager offered me a job.

"Welcome aboard!" he said. "And welcome to the family!"

Speaking of the family, my parents had less enthused reactions when I called to inform them of my new, gainful employment. My father pointed out that *technically* I'd be working on Broadway, but my mother yammered on about my six-figure college tuition. "Do you know what that money could've done in my Roth IRA?!" she screamed. "I mean, if you were going to wait tables, *fine*! But then *why* did we have to spend all that money on that goddamn BFA?!" She stayed on this tirade for a good twenty minutes before arriving at her old standby. "Well, I guess the upshot is, at least you didn't call to tell me you had cancer. Speaking of which: Does the Olive Garden provide health insurance?"

The Olive Garden does not provide health insurance. The Olive Garden does, however, require you to wear a uniform of pleated slacks and tie. And the Olive Garden does require you to wear a name tag. You're forced to pin it on your shapeless button-down shirt so you can spend the next six hours thinking, *Why are name tags only required at exactly those jobs where you'd most like to remain anonymous?* This way, all your customers can screech for you by name. And what's more and better still, on the occasions wherein people you knew from high school or college wander in for a bite en route to a Broadway matinee, they'll be able to know for sure that it's you.

"There's Sara Barron!" they'll say. "All grown up and waiting tables in a tie!"

My first week on the job I got summoned over to a table of four fifty-ish adults, two men and two women. The women wore *Mamma Mia!* T-shirts, the men, Dallas Cowboys jerseys, and all four sported visors that read NEW YORK FUCKIN' CITY. I have a deep-seated fear of adults who wear matching headwear, but as an Olive Garden waiter, I had no choice but to talk to them.

"Hey there," I said, "can I get you guys started with something to drink?"

Instead of answering my question directly, one of the women (I'll call her Regina-Sue since she sure did look the part of a two-name Southern belle gone bad) pointed at the specials card and screamed, "WHAT'S THIS?!"

The "THIS" she'd asked after was guanciale, an item featured in that evening's special pasta. It was, I thought, a fair question. (One might wonder, "What, while eating out, constitutes an *un*fair question?" A brief sampling includes: "Can you run outside and fill my meter?" or, with dirty diaper in hand, "Can you toss this for me?") I was well aware that if I hadn't spent the last week memorizing cooking methods and ingredients, had I not recently become more well versed in pig product than I'd ever hoped to be, I certainly wouldn't know what guanciale was either. So I told Regina-Sue, "Guanciale is pork cheek."

Some waiters like to go the euphemistic route with menu descriptions, but not me. I believe customers should be well informed about what it is they're about to eat. I wouldn't want some unsuspecting vegetarian to order the wrong thing and then vomit out of horror and disgust. Would that turn of events amuse me *in theory*? Sure. But if I'm at work and there's a public upchuck situation, guess who's got to clean it up? The back waiter, Jose-Manuel, and I are flipping a coin, I'll tell you that much.

So I told Regina-Sue: Guanciale = Pork + Cheek, and Regina-Sue answered back by asking, "Is that then vegetarian?"

The question both fascinated and confused me. I couldn't decide on the best way to reply.

Should I keep it simple? Should I say, "No, actually, it's not"?

Or should I go the riskier route of asking if she was retarded? "Now, Ms. Regina-Sue," I'd scold, "did you just ask if pig cheek was vegetarian? Are you retarded?"

But with the latter option, while she *may* have slapped me jovially on the back and told me to "go on and scoot" after another raspberry iced tea, she could just as likely howl after a manager and in so doing get me fired. Of course her NEW YORK FUCKIN' CITY visor *did* suggest a fantastic sense of humor, but one can never be too sure.

I decided the best thing to do would be to repeat myself. So again I told Regina-Sue, and I said each syllable very slowly this time, "PORK. CHEEK. IS. FROM. A. PIG."

"So no?" she repeated. "Not vegetarian?"

"No," I affirmed. "*Not* vegetarian." Then I inched away from the table to give them more time with the menu.

Later that same week I was out to dinner with friends. I said, "Oh, get a load of this!" and relayed my guanciale story to the lot of them. This one girl named Phoebe, a trust-fund twenty-something without a day's worth of experience in the restaurant industry, refused to believe me. She rolled her eyes and said, "You're *obviously* exaggerating."

The accusation shocked me. When I'd told the same anecdote to my coworker Justin, he didn't bat an eye. He'd said only, "Oh, I've heard that one before. Was she wearing anything to advertise a Broadway musical?" I mentioned the *Mamma Mia!* T-shirt. "Well, there you go," he said, "she'll be just the tip of your iceberg."

Justin was my only friend at the Olive Garden. Homosexual, and with a left eye made lazy by hallucinogenic drugs, I found him far more interesting than the rest of the crew. He'd fallen into waitering after failing as an actor, and to pass the time we liked to trade audition horror stories:

> SARA: *I once read a scene from* Angels in America *with a man with halitosis.*
>
> JUSTIN: I *once read a scene from* A Streetcar Named Desire *with a woman who was cross-eyed!*
>
> SARA: *I once watched my ex-boyfriend dig through garbage in a clown suit.*
>
> JUSTIN: I *once watched my ex-boyfriend sing "Puttin' on the Ritz" in a tuxedo.*
>
> SARA: *That's not that bad.*
>
> JUSTIN: *It was in a conference room. For an audience of five.*

I adored Justin for his stories, but also because we shared a deep aversion to Freddo, the Olive Garden's manager. "Oh, dear god," were the first words Justin ever said to me. "Freddo's playing air guitar near table forty-one. Excuse me while I vomit."

Freddo was the one in the tight pewter slacks who'd hired me thanks to my self-described "vivacious personality." He hailed from Staten Island and loved high fives and the verb form of the word *rock,* as in "That rocks!" At the end of an evening, he'd charge toward whichever waiter had earned the highest number in alcohol sales and scream, "THAT ROCKS! GIVE IT UP!" to solicit a double high five. This made me the only waiter in the entire Western Hemisphere who preferred an iced-tea sale to that of a twelve-dollar cocktail. It may have meant I raked in fewer tips, but that was well worth it to keep my boss from coming at me with pit stains like pancakes.

Per Justin's comment, Freddo also loved the air guitar. I, conversely, have a severe allergy to it. I don't get hives or experience shortness of breath, but when I'm exposed, I do experience extreme and immediate vaginal dryness. And Justin's remark that air guitar made *him* want to vomit meant we had something over which to bond: a shared aversion, albeit one that manifested itself in very different ways.

My favorite night to work at the Olive Garden was Monday. It was Freddo's night off and business was usually slow, and this allowed Justin and me to engage in more lengthy conversations. He'd regale me with stories from the oeuvre he'd titled "The Most Psychotic Customers."

"One of my faves," he once said, "was this lovely older woman I encountered six years ago while working at another midtown restaurant. She was at the beginning of a luncheon with six of her friends, when all of sudden she waved me over to the table. The second I got over there, she started shouting, 'WHAT'S THE "QUICKIE" OF THE DAY?' I had no idea what she was talking about. So I said, 'I beg your pardon?' Well, then she got *really* angry at having to ask twice and yelled even louder this time, 'HERE!' while pointing to the specials card. 'THE QUICKIE!'"

It was only with the aid of the menu that Justin was finally able to understand the question: The woman wanted to know what was in the daily quiche.

A greener waiter might have balked, but Justin answered concisely and without a hint of the condescension to which he was entitled, "The 'quickie' Lorraine," he explained, "contains ham and Swiss cheese."

As if that wasn't enough, this same woman forced him to field another doozy upon his presentation of the check. "HEY, YOU!" she screamed once he'd laid it on the table. "NO ONE HERE ORDERED A THIRTY-FIVE-DOLLAR GRA-TWIT-TITTIE!"

Justin took a moment to consider how best to handle the situation. While it would have been gratifying to say, "You're dumb; here's why . . . ," then go on to grace her with a detailed explanation, he realized he didn't actually want to disrupt her ignorance. He knew it would bring such joy and laughter to all the waiters in her future. He didn't want to rob them of the opportunity to tell their own story of the woman in the *Blossom* hat who lunched in midtown, who knew nothing of service charges, who pronounced *quiche* "quickie," as though it were not a savory pie but a fast and furious sex encounter.

So Justin said only, "Ma'am, the 'gra-twit-tittie' just means that the tip has been included. We do it for all parties of six or more."

"Then she called me a 'lazy idiot,'" Justin concluded, "for 'stealing' her 'hard-earned money.' Well, that was my breaking point. I said, 'Ma'am, you're—what? Fifty pounds overweight? Sixty maybe?—and parading around Manhattan in a denim one-piece and a *Blossom* hat? One of the two of us here might be "lazy" and an "idiot," but it sure as shit ain't me,' and then I got fired. Not even for calling her fat, which I *did* feel bad about, but because I said the word *shit*. Or, as my nineteen-year-old manager referred to it, because I 'lacked good judgment.'"

Justin's anecdote illustrates a noteworthy aspect of waiting tables: You're harassed constantly on both sides. From the customers *and* the management. I was harassed constantly by Freddo, who liked to snag my attention by grabbing at my hipbone with the sweaty palm of his hand. From someone less physically reminiscent of Wallace Shawn, I might've warmed to the action, but coming from Freddo, it succeeded only in kicking the vaginal dryness into gear. I was also harassed by the Olive Garden customers. I was harassed in many different ways for many different reasons, but most frequently regarding the issue of decaffeinated coffee. People got hysterical over it. Mosnu was the coffee maker at the Olive Garden, the person whose job it was to make and deliver the coffees after the waiters had taken the order. One night I saw him get assaulted by a pregnant woman. I'd been in the midst of taking an order when I'd felt a frantic tapping on my back from Jose-Manuel, the back waiter. "Mami!" he cried. "Very big lady table twenty-one is angry lady! Her talking crazy! Hitting Mosnu!" Then he demonstrated said hitting by swatting at my arm. "You go? Make better?"

As the waiter in charge of table 21 it was my job to go and speak with the angry pregnant lady. I told Jose-Manuel, "Don't worry, I'll handle it. Just remember: She, too, shall pass." Jose-Manuel and I spent forty hours a week together, and I'd always tell him the same thing when confronted with demented customer antics: "He/she, too, shall pass. Let us pray for food poisoning. Let us pray Arturo didn't wash his hands after butchering the pig and went straight to the greens for the 'garden fresh' salad. Amen."

I inched carefully toward the woman, who, as Jose-Manuel had warned, was screaming and thrashing her hands around.

"Ma'am, is there something I can help you with?" I asked.

"WELL, I JUST ASKED *HIM*," she screamed, and pointed at Mosnu, "WHETHER OR NOT THIS IS DECAF! AND HE JUST SHAKES HIS HEAD LIKE AN IDIOT, LIKE HE DOESN'T UNDERSTAND!"

I turned to Mosnu. "Definitely decaf?" I asked. He nodded. I turned back toward her. "It's decaf," I said. "Definitely decaf. You'll be fine."

"WELL, IT BETTER BE!" she threatened. "'CAUSE IF IT'S NOT, YOU BETTER BELIEVE I'LL CALL YOUR HOUSE AT THREE A.M. TO TELL YOU SO!"

It was shocking, the number of people who issued this same threat of the late-night phone call. And more shocking still that they all seemed to think themselves amusing and/or original for having done so. In the early days of my Olive Garden career, I'd respond by mustering a half grin or a weak "ha-ha." I did, at first, *try* to gather the energy to care about a stranger's good night's sleep. But after enough 13 percent tips for remade cappuccinos and grown adults for whom the words *please* and *thank you* were as foreign as something said in ancient Greek, I traded in my sympathy card for a sarcastic retort. I started saying, "Well, call if you like. I work nights, so I'll be up. Oh, wait! That's right! You don't have my number. Anyway, enjoy your 'decaf' latte." And when I said the word *decaf,* I'd use quotation marks just to keep them guessing.

I never actually made a drink with caffeine when it had been ordered without. *Supposedly* some people are allergic to it, and I wanted revenge but not necessarily a homicide on my hands. I wished discomfort and disease, crabs and various types of fungus on the masses. But not actual death. Early in my Olive Garden training, I'd attended a mandatory seminar on food allergies and was forced to watch a video called *Ignorance Kills: A Restaurant Guide to Allergy Awareness.* The opening shot was of a girl who died from a peanut allergy after having been misinformed about a cookie. They kept showing the mom sobbing atop her daughter's tombstone. It was as pleasant as you might expect, being forced to watch that video, but I'll give it to the producers that they succeeded in getting their message across. They also made me realize that I didn't actually want to kill people. I felt good about that realization. I felt good knowing that no matter how bad waiting tables got, no matter how much of the dark side of humanity I was forced to confront day in and day out, I hadn't yet turned homicidal.

I had a very particular fantasy about how my Olive Garden tenure would end. I imagined that one day I'd get a call from the casting offices at *Sex and the City* telling me I'd booked a recurring role, one that involved sex scenes with John Corbett and a six-figure paycheck. Later that same afternoon, I'd march proudly into work to make a grand display of quitting. I'd toss my orthopedic shoes in the garbage. "I won't be needing *these* anymore," I'd say as I untied my apron, "or *this*." Some coworkers would clap and smile; others would glower, green with envy. All the managers would say, "From the first time we met you, we've been saying you seemed bound for better things. We're not surprised. We wish you the best of luck." Maybe they'd throw something in about always being welcomed back with open arms. Freddo would refrain from high fiving and/or grabbing at my hipbones. I'd promise to remember them "when" (i.e., following forthcoming stardom), then I'd walk out the front door as a gust of wind blew gently through my hair to make it look full bodied.

I had to settle instead on being fired after a series of customer complaints. They all complained about my attitude. They called it "a problem." In the instance with Regina–"Is Pig Cheek Vegetarian?"–Sue, I'd held back from asking if she was retarded because I'd only been at the Olive Garden a week and didn't want to rock the boat. But as time wore on, my patience wore thin. While I don't recall ever asking someone directly if they were retarded, I did become increasingly short-tempered. You'd do the same if forced to clean up toddler vomit three times a week because parents let their children indulge in pig-sized portions of fettuccini Alfredo. Enough instances wherein you're yelled at for prices over which you lack control, enough anorexics in hysterics over the paltry selection of "lite" items, enough drunk men hurling check presenters at your head for having been charged for the ice cream that their child didn't like, and you can actually feel the process of your fuse getting shorter. After six months on the job, even less inane questions did me in:

"So how about the Venetian apricot chicken," someone might ask. "Do you think it's any good?"

"It is if you like chicken," I'd respond. "If you like it slathered in jelly and covered in a shroud of wilted greens, then I think you'll think it's good. If not, then not."

Or "What do you recommend?"

This one killed me: What did I "recommend?" I recommend not having dinner at the Olive Garden. I recommend *not* asking for recommendations at places where waiters wear name tags.

The straw that finally broke the Sara's back was a forty-something woman dining solo. I'll call her "Grandma" since, over the course of an hour, she'd prove to be the only person I'd ever met more difficult than my grandma. So Grandma came in for lunch one afternoon and ordered the herb-grilled salmon. She took a few bites and then started screaming. "MISS! EXCUSE ME, MISS! *MISS!*"

I was in the midst of carrying a tray of Coors Lights to a nearby table, so I nodded at her wordlessly, giving the look that waiters give their customers to say, *I see you; I hear you; I'll be with you in just a minute.*

But that wasn't good enough for Grandma. *"MISS!!"* she screamed again. "I *NEED* TO SPEAK WITH YOU!"

I think the most dangerous adage to indulge is this: The Squeaky Wheel Gets the Grease. It validates an endless stream of complaints and in so doing teaches the lesson that whining like a spoiled pig is an effective course of action. I try to fight that. I try to do my part to let the public know: These antics don't work. When a word like *now!* gets shouted in my face by an adult, I will not jump to complete the task at hand. What I will do is inch with excruciating slowness toward the offending party. I'll stop along the way to retie my orthopedics, apply Chap Stick, stop for a chat with a coworker. These antics piss the tits off most people, just as I intend them to.

"This place is a joke!" they wail in response. "We're NEVER coming back!"

"Thank *god*," I reply. "See you never."

So I walked as slowly as I could toward Grandma's table. "Yes?" I asked. "Is something wrong?"

"THIS!" she screamed, pointing at her plate of salmon. "IT TASTES FISHY!"

"That's because it's fish," I said.

Grandma had already pushed too many of my buttons to warrant a more in-depth response. She'd slapped my hand as I refilled her water (she hadn't wanted ice; ice hurt her teeth) and requested a salad in lieu of the complimentary Olive Garden bread sticks. "The bread sticks make my mouth feel funny," she'd whined. "I want something else."

I didn't have the energy to deal, frankly, and so after explaining that food made with fish will tend to taste like fish, I turned around to walk away. This dismissal irritated Grandma. "Don't you get an attitude with me!" she yelled.

"You make it hard not to," I replied.

This sentence also irritated Grandma. I wasn't giving her an inch and she wanted someone who would. "I want a manager!" she screamed, and turned toward Justin who'd strolled by to see what the fuss was about. "Can I get a manager?"

"It's 'may I,'" he corrected. "'May I get a manager.' And yes, of course you may."

The grammar correction pushed Grandma over the edge, and by the time Freddo arrived to assuage her, she'd started foaming at the mouth. I stood beside him as he tried to mediate.

"THE WAITRESS WAS INCREDIBLY RUDE!" she howled. "I DIDN'T GO OUT TO LUNCH TO PAY GOOD MONEY TO HAVE SOMEONE BE RUDE TO ME!"

"I'm sure you didn't," I piped in. "But the piece of the puzzle that you're missing is this: *You* were rude first."

There's a cause-effect relationship that restaurant customers tend to overlook. Namely, the understanding that service with a smile is a response, not a guarantee. I'll dole it out happily in return for decent manners, but if someone slaps my hand, then whines about the fishy taste of salmon, service with a smile is a no-go. ~~Grandma got bitchy, waiter got bitchy. Cause and effect.~~ It all seemed logical enough to me.

Not to Freddo, though. And not to Grandma, either. The second I said, "You were rude first," she whipped her head toward Freddo and asked if he was going to let me talk to her like that.

"No, ma'am," he cooed, "of course not." Then he offered her an Olive Garden gift certificate—"It's the least I can do"—and a refund for her meal. All *I* received for *my* troubles, on the other hand, was a stern look and the instruction to meet him in his office after my shift.

My mother says that when you get overwhelmed with anger, you ought to diffuse it by picturing your antagonist naked. A standard approach, but here I took it a step further by zoning in on Freddo's bean-sized balls. This was juvenile, I know. But it made the proceeding twenty minutes easier to bear.

"We had this episode tonight and three complaints the week before," he said later after work, "and last week you showed up an hour late to your Thursday shift."

I *had* shown up an hour late, but that was because I'd nabbed an audition for Excedrin, and it ended up running later than expected. And I couldn't very well put the demands of a corporate waiter job before those more creative pursuits of Excedrin salesmanship, now could I? I expressed these sentiments to Freddo, who sighed and leaned forward on his elbows.

"You know, Sara, I'm starting to think you don't really want to be here."

There was the understatement of the decade. "That's because I don't," I said. "I've got bills to pay like the rest of us but I certainly don't *want* to be here." The notion that other folks felt otherwise struck me as very, very strange. "Do you? Does anyone?"

That's when Freddo told me to get off my high horse and pack up my things. It wasn't the sort of positive fanfare I'd imagined, although the sudden realization that I'd never bear witness to his air guitar again did add an element of victory. I tossed my name tag in the garbage, my apron in the hamper, my orthopedics in my backpack (they'd cost a hundred dollars; they weren't going any-where), and rounded the corner of Forty-seventh Street and Broadway. Sure enough, a gentle gust of wind *did* blow through my hair. Although instead of adding body, it served only to mess up my bangs.

IN NEW YORK, some people hear *the Olive Garden* and think: *midtown nightmare.* Others think: *rehearsal dinner.* Years ago, the marketing genius behind the company wanted to broaden the appeal and created the slogan "The Olive Garden: When you're here, you're family." It's got a nice ring to it but con-veniently omits the details of exactly what kind of family it is that you're about to join. The campaign suggests a boisterous Sicilian bunch with phenomenal culinary flair, a jovial Grandma Giovanna who speaks only broken English as she kneads her famous meat-balls. The reality, sadly, is very, very different. It revolves around diversified tourists, orthopedic-clad waiters, and a throng of sweaty management who mistakenly thinks the "family" "rocks."

people are unappealing

After getting fired from the Olive Garden, I filed for unemployment because I liked the idea of collecting money second only to the idea of not having to work. "That sounds *amazing*!" I said to Maggie after she suggested it. "I should have done this years ago!" But after three weeks without daily human interaction, three weeks spent couch-bound, I began to reconsider. There was one afternoon I caught myself talking to my coffee mug— "Hello!" I'd said. "Are you afraid of germs?"—and then another wherein I hallucinated that my FUPA started singing Barbra Streisand.

"Pee-pullll," I heard. *"Pee-pul who need pee-pul . . . are the LUCKIEST PEE-PUL . . . in the woooooorld . . ."*

The day your fat upper-pussy area has something to say about your fundamental human needs is the day you must take action. You must facilitate change. For me, it forced a realization that unemployment and I might not be the greatest fit.

At the time, I was dating a man named Darren. Darren also

worked in restaurants, except instead of waiting tables, he cooked slabs of expensive meat at an upscale joint in downtown Manhattan. We'd met several months before at a bedbug-infested loft party in Williamsburg, Brooklyn, and had been dating ever since, primarily because we had similar work schedules. The restaurant Darren worked at did fantastic business because it had a celebrity chef at its helm, and as people love celebrities, they'd go to the restaurant in droves in the hope of snagging a look at him. (I don't feel comfortable revealing the chef's identity, not because celebploitation is beneath me—on the contrary, I'd relish the opportunity—but because with $47.09 in my bank account at present, I can't afford a lawsuit. So in lieu of doing so, I'll use a pseudonym. I'll call him "Luigi." Luigi the Celebrity Chef. And in lieu of revealing the name of Luigi's restaurant, I'll call it, simply, "Hell.")

After the solitude of unemployment drove me to the aforementioned FUPA hallucinations, I asked Darren to help me get a job at Hell. Unqualified though I may have been for the transition from one- to three-star dining, Darren did as requested. Darren *always* did as requested because on our third date, after drinking a bottle of bourbon, he confessed a desire to perform oral sex on other men. A divulgence like this would not have surprised me had it come from any number of my former actor flames, but from a guy like Darren, who wore a backward baseball cap and addressed other men exclusively as "dude," it was shocking. Now I'm not the blackmailing type per se, but Darren hadn't known me very long and didn't seem to want to take the chance. He let slip, "There's something about doing oral stuff with other dudes that really turns me on," and after that when I said, "Jump," he asked, "How high?" When I asked, "Can you get me an interview at Hell?" he answered, "You got it, babe"—Darren always called me "babe"—"just name a time."

I showed up early to my interview snugged into a pair of dark-wash Old Navy jeans, rambled on about the "importance" of "quality customer service," and they offered me a job. You'd think being back in an apron and orthopedic shoes would have sucked me of my will to live, but I felt surprisingly optimistic about the whole thing. And frankly, I had the Olive Garden to thank for that. (It's like cancer that way: It helps to put things in perspective.) Hell may not have been my John-Corbett-sex-scene dream job, but it *was* a step up in the class department. I appreciated this. I appreciated that the average customer's meal began with carafes of expensive Italian wine in lieu of raspberry iced teas. I appreciated the decrease in fanny packs atop the clientele. I appreciated the absence of children and bread sticks. But every silver lining has to have its cloud, and Hell was no exception. The experience of working for a celebrity chef had the aforementioned advantages, but with each small improvement came a whole new set of problems. Because celebrity begets celebrity, a significant percentage of the clientele was other famous people. This was fun at first, and also it was helpful in answering a question that had been plaguing me for years: Why do celebrities insist on discussing how they're "just like everybody else"?

Eva Longoria: "I'm absolutely normal . . . just like everybody else!"

Jennifer Lopez: "Basically, I'm just like anybody else!"

Gisele Bündchen: "I'm a normal person!"

Working at Hell I realized it's because they all surround themselves with a motley crew of more celebrities. If you spent three nights a week noshing on thirty-dollar plates of pasta in a Tory Burch dress as your driver waited outside *and* your best friends did the same, you'd start to think that's normal too. Luigi, for example, socialized exclusively with others of his same status and exposure level; he preferred film actors and internationally renowned musicians, but in a pinch, any household name sufficed. A night at work felt like watching a red-carpet stroll. If, that is, the event to necessitate the carpet was one called "Who's the Most Entitled?"

This is not to say all famous folks were rude. On the contrary, many seemed to understand that with all eyes cast upon them, they should at least perform "well mannered." The more specific problem was that none of them understood the word *no:* Drop that N-bomb, and they'd stare back at you with a look not so much of horror, but rather of confusion. One night the son of a very famous musician came in for dinner; I'll call him Stella McCartney since his name isn't really Stella McCartney. Anyway, Stella McCartney was dissatisfied with the music being played. He told me to change it.

"Excuse me, miss?" he'd said. I walked over. "This music you're playing sucks. Can you change it for me? Thanks."

Music was one thing we couldn't change in accordance with celebrity preferences because they all wanted something different: Celebrity #1 thought the music was too frenetic, celebrity #2 found it too depressing, etc., and so I quickly memorized a stock response. Whenever the subject came up, I'd affect a subtly condescending tone and say, "We can't accommodate everyone's needs since we get requests for different music all the time. But the iPod's on shuffle, so don't worry: We'll be on to something different soon."

I gave Stella McCartney my memorized response. He looked confused and said, "So you'll change it?"

"Sir," I tried again, "I'm sorry, but I can't."

"Look, I don't mean to be an asshole . . ." People who say this never mean it. What they mean is: I know I'm being an asshole, but I don't care to admit it. Not to you, and not to myself. "The thing is," he continued, "I'm a musician and I *know* music, and I'm telling you: The music you've got on is *bad.* So just do me a favor and change it, okay? Thanks."

"You're welcome!" I said, and walked away.

I didn't intend to fulfill his request, but there comes a time in a certain kind of conversation with a certain type of person where you have to make the choice to disengage. You have to recognize you're in a losing battle. Here, I lied and spoon-fed Stella McCartney "You're welcome!" figuring I'd deal with the consequences later. And I did. They came when I dropped the check on the table. Stella McCartney slammed his black Amex card atop it, then on his signed receipt left me an 8 percent tip and the following note: "Awful service." Perhaps I should've been offended, but I was too busy feeling thrilled by his departure.

For the next seventy-two hours, I actually enjoyed waiting tables. It's rare I ever *enjoy* waiting tables, but the thing about dealing with Stella McCartney was that he made me feel appreciative of every moment of my job wherein I wasn't forced to deal with him. For three days straight, I had this glass-half-full smile slapped across my face. On the fourth day, however, Stella McCartney came back. The sight of him standing at the maître d' stand felt like a punch to the stomach. I felt shock, then pain, then anger. "WHAT?! HOW?! WHY?!" I screamed at Lulu, my seasoned Dominican coworker. "I thought I'd gotten rid of him!" Not only that, I'd *shown off* about having gotten rid of him to all my fellow waiters—they'd applauded my efforts and relished the detail of him using his "musician" status to validate his music tastes—and now here he was again to shame me!

Lulu gently laid a hand atop my shoulder. "They do that all the time," she said. "All these celebrities. You have to think of them as babies: They'll have a tantrum, but ten minutes later they've totally forgotten why."

On this second visit Stella McCartney had his iPod with him. "Excuse me, miss?" he started. "Do me a favor and hook in my iPod, would you? Thanks. The music'll be better that way. Thanks."

I saw where this was going and lacked the energy to follow. So what I did was, I *mimed* taking Stella McCartney's iPod without *actually* taking it. Then I scurried away before he'd registered my crafty ploy. This method of avoidance worked well enough until, of course, it didn't. Until I had to walk past his table again. That's when he shouted, "YOU DIDN'T TAKE THE IPOD!"

"Really?" I asked. "Are you sure? That's weird, I thought I did."

Then he leaned toward me and struggled, it seemed, to affect a tone more foreboding than hysterical. "Listen," he seethed, "Luigi is a friend of mine. And you better believe he'll find out about this."

PEOPLE ARE UNAPPEALING

Perhaps I should've started shaking in my orthopedic boots, but I couldn't take him seriously. I fielded this same threat all the time, and what the celebrity loons failed to understand was that their "good friend" Luigi was the one who put their hated rules into effect in the first place. Luigi was the one who'd said we wouldn't change the music. Luigi was the one who refused to let us modify the menu. This last point proved especially difficult for a slew of famous actresses, one of whom appeared one night in an expensive camisole and oversize boho sweater on a quest for steamed halibut. "Do you have anything lighter than what's listed on the menu?" she asked. "Can I get a fillet of steamed halibut and a side of veggies?"

A word to the wise about dieting: For your next meal out, don't go upscale Italian. Don't go to a restaurant with a preponderance of meat, cheese, and dough on the menu. Luigi's menu consisted of little else, and the small selection of fish and vegetables he did include (*vegetables*, I say, not *veggies*; those of us over five must unite in opposition to the latter option) had been soaked preemptively in duck fat and oil. There wasn't so much as a steamer in sight in the kitchen, so I told the cami-sporting actress no. She looked confused.

"What?" she asked.

"No," I answered.

"No?" she said.

"No," I said.

"Look, I'm not trying to be an asshole or anything . . ."

"Of course not."

". . . it's just that I'd *really* like some veggies. And halibut. And just so you know—and I'm not trying to be an asshole or anything—but I *am* a good friend of Luigi's."

"Of course," I replied. "But there's still not halibut or a steamer in the kitchen."

The cami-sporter's cheeks got flushed. "WELL THAT'S RETARDED!" she roared. She was finished with her game of feigned politeness. "Is Luigi here? I want to talk to him directly."

197

"He's not," I answered back. Celebrity chefs are rarely at their restaurants. They're kept busy at the Food Network or on the road promoting products like a signature ladle or barbecue sauce. "Luigi's in Aspen guest-judging *Top Chef*."

"Well, I'm calling him now," she warned, and reached into the pocket of her boho sweater for her iPhone. "What's your name?"

"Crystal," I answered, "Crystal St. James. Make sure to tell him I said hi."

I saw celebrities on a regular basis, so over time I got desensitized. I couldn't be easily intimidated since it was just like Lulu said: None of them remembered to follow through on their threats anyway. So why cower? The list of celebrities who could awe me into silence or subservience started shrinking day by day. I would've said Gwen Stefani, but then I saw Gwen Stefani and then my interest waned. I would've said Jake Gyllenhaal, but then I saw Jake Gyllenhaal and then my interest waned. I would've said Kirsten Dunst . . . and so on. After a month on the job my list of "Who Could Still Impress Me" had shrunk to five. They were, in no particular order:

1. John Stamos
2. Oprah Winfrey
3. Stephen Sondheim
4. Britney Spears

Of course, that list includes just four, and that's because the fifth deserves special mention. The fifth was the front man of a band I'd idolized since 1991, and were this anecdote about to take a turn for the flattering, I'd refer to him by name. Instead, I'll call him "Twat Waffle." I must give credit where credit is due for his pseudonym, and that's to the waiters and cooks at Hell who first screamed it into being. The story goes that Twat Waffle once showed up with his entourage—and this was all before my time at Hell—for a five-course meal at 11:55 P.M. Come three A.M., he was still going strong and hungry for waffles. Blueberry ones. And the thing was, the pastry department at Hell had this waffle maker because they served artisanal gelato in homemade waffle cones, and so they had to follow through with his request. The cooks had to scrounge through the kitchen for the proper ingredients to whip up a decent batter while the waiter had to run to the nearest twenty-four-hour bodega to buy a pint of blueberries.

"Fucking twat," said the waiter.

"Fucking waffles," said a cook. And so it was. The name caught like fire on a dry toupee and stuck.

One month into Hell, however, and I knew none of this. All I did know was that Twat Waffle's sensitive, poetic lyrics and melodious tunes addressing subjects as complex as Love! and Pain! and Loneliness! had, on occasions too numerous to count, been the balm on my tween-through-teenage angst. The chance to see him in person was thrilling and stayed thrilling in the face of my otherwise encompassing desensitization.

Darren and I were walking into work one afternoon when I heard the happy news that Twat Waffle and Luigi were friends. Darren started whining, "Tonight's gonna suck. Twat Waffle's coming in."

"Twat Waffle?!" I repeated, and stopped in my tracks. "*Twat Waffle* Twat Waffle?!"

"Jesus Christ," sighed Darren, "can't you walk and talk at the same time?" I shot him a look that said, I'm *the one who knows you're bi-curious. You best simmer down.* He apologized and playfully swatted at my ass. "Sorry, babe. You're friggin' *awesome.* You know I think you're awesome." Darren went on to explain that Twat Waffle had made frequent appearances in Hell ever since he and Luigi got friendly at something like a fund-raiser—he wasn't sure of the details—and Luigi approached Twat Waffle to say, "Hey, man, I just wanted to say thank you. For all the years of awesome fucking music." And Twat Waffle answered, "Hey, man, thank *you.* Your food is fucking genius." Then some other nondescript, metaphoric dick-sucking occurred, and after that they were as attached at the hip as two on-the-road celebrities could be.

They'd even shot an episode of that idiotic, short-lived TV series *Iconoclast* in which two celebrity friends hang out and each talk about how brilliant and influential the other is.

Darren's Twat Waffle aversion confused me. Sure, I despise using the word *genius* as an adjective as much as the next person, but the story of Twat Waffle having done so was hearsay! I couldn't believe he'd be capable of such pomposity. I couldn't believe anyone would feel anything but reverence in his presence.

"Well, believe it," Darren urged. "The dude is nothing but a '90s has-been who validates his shitty slice of celebrity by showing up after hours at a restaurant and keeping a bunch of guys in a kitchen who've already worked a twelve-hour day. He's a prick, babe, trust me."

I couldn't, though. You don't write songs about the shared experience of human suffering, then act the douche, correct? Correct. I decided to check Darren's accusations against Lulu's more even-keeled and astute opinions, but I didn't get that far. I started out by saying, "Is it true Twat Waffle comes in here a lot? Because Darren—" but then she whipped around to face me with a look of terror so dramatic, I stopped talking.

"Did you just say, 'Twat Waffle'?" she asked. I nodded. "He's coming here?" Her voice was full of terror and foreboding, the kind you might affect if your doctor said *malignant.* "He's coming here *tonight*?"

"That's what Darren said."

"MOTHERFUCKER!" she screamed. "MOTHER*FUCKER*-FUCKER!"

Lulu's wailings set in motion a chain of waiter inquiries as to what all the fuss was about, and upon hearing the Twat Waffle answer, the word *fuck* Ping-Ponged all across the dining room:

WAITER 2: *What?*

WAITER 1: *Twat Waffle!*

WAITER 2: *Fuck!*

WAITER 3: *What?*

WAITER 2: *Twat Waffle!*

WAITER 3: *Fuck!*

until everyone, each waiter and back waiter, a cluster of line cooks, and a number of the less professional managers and sommeliers, had joined in the chorus of despair. What everyone was so upset about, it seemed, was that because Twat Waffle always showed up after hours, his presence—as demonstrated by his namesake debacle—guaranteed a sixteen-hour workday not only for the kitchen staff, but for the one waiter and manager who'd have to stick around to serve him. Or, as my coworkers referred to it, "to deal." "Oh god. Oh god," moaned Lulu as she paced in circles and cracked her knuckles. "I can't deal with him. I can't fucking deal with him. Not again, god. Not again . . ." On any given night at Hell, there were only five waiters working, and a 20 percent chance the ax might fall seemed too much for anyone to bear.

When you work in a restaurant, you must endure these things called "pre-meals." They happen before the start of service, and managers use them to harp on asinine activities like "up-sells" and/or "product familiarity." And at a place like Hell, where celebrities flew through the door faster than you could say, "Liev Schreiber is *so* rude to waiters!" they're also used to review the reservation book and prepare for noteworthy appearances.

"All right," was the opener to that night's pre-meal. "So for those of you who haven't heard, Twat Waffle *is* coming in." Cue deafening, guttural moans. "Save it. It's only getting worse: He's not scheduled to get here until about midnight or twelve-thirty-ish so one of you will have to stay and deal. We can draw straws or someone can volunteer. Your choice."

I surprised myself and raised my hand. "Um, I'll do it," I said. "That's no problem."

If I was someone selfless enough to take care of something like a dog—let's say I was suddenly a dog owner—I would sooner throw that dog out into the recyclables section of my apartment's communal Dumpster than I would adopt the mantra "Take One for the Team." It's simply not how I (as the kids these days are saying) "like to roll"; I cannot "roll that way." I wasn't being altruistic. I volunteered because I thought waiting on Twat Waffle sounded like fun. The staff at Hell—Every. Single. Person.—may have said strong words to the contrary, but stronger still was my twelve-year-long idolization. Embittered waiter though I may have been, the chance to fill his water glass got me feeling giddy as a gal of twenty-one! I imagined us making eye contact! I imagined we'd share some flash of understanding as I placed his glass of chardonnay beside him! *She's not just another fan,* he'd think, *not just another waiter. No. She gets me.* That *girl really gets me.* If that didn't happen, well, at least I'd be guaranteed the chance to see him in person and at least I'd make some extra cash to invest in my face-waxing fund. (People are always surprised when they find out how often I must remove my facial hair. You wouldn't think it because I'm relatively pale, but the fact of the matter is that I'm covered in this centimeter-long tangle of peach-colored scruff. I spend a thousand bucks a year so men won't describe me as fuzzy. So their friends won't say, "Whoa. You mean fuzzy like, mentally? Like she's not that alert?" And my guy would have to answer, "No! I mean fuzzy like *physically* fuzzy! Like she's *covered* in . . . fuzz! Fuzz, dude, fuzz!")

Waiters in New York tend not to be the most religious bunch, but when I volunteered to be the one to stay to wait on Twat Waffle, this group got downright reverential. I felt Pope-ish. There were a lot of hands thrown up to god, a lot of people blessing me. Lulu got teary eyed. "Oh, thank you!" she exulted. "Thank you so much!" Then they started offering to buy me beer, which isn't something I imagine happens often for the Pope, but I welcomed the perk nonetheless. *No wonder people like this gift-of-giving stuff,* I thought. (I still wasn't convinced of the point of benevolence for benevolence's sake, but good gosh! When people gave you credit for it? How exciting!) The eight hours that passed between pre-meal and Twat Waffle's arrival did so without incident. I *did* have to field this one customer who got plastered and encouraged my manager to fire me for "not looking Italian," and I *did* have to watch the lead singer of Maroon 5 clutch a wineglass like a six-year-old, but that was it.

Twat Waffle arrived at 12:42 A.M., forty-two minutes after the kitchen had closed to the public. Hell was a big restaurant with a long hallway leading to a massive back dining room with large round tables in the corners where celebrities would sit when they came in for dinner, and Twat Waffle slinking down that hallway looked, first of all, as if he thought he was playing the part of the Fonz on *Happy Days*—he was walking like the Fonz—but also as if he'd just competed in a boxing match. By this I mean he wore a hoodie with the hood up and a small white towel over his shoulder. Darren, having poked his head out of the kitchen, would later explain that this was because Twat Waffle had just played a concert at Madison Square Garden and he hadn't yet stopped sweating.

Also, Twat Waffle wore Bono-y sunglasses that weren't at all boxer-ish, just affected. I understand some famous people sport the shades to afford themselves the anonymity they worked so hard to shirk the years before the fame befell them, but that's not what was going on here. No. These were after-hours shades paired with a flamboyant Fonzie sort of side-step, paired with a towel, paired with an entourage of gaunt homosexuals all in matching fedoras and Ray-Bans. It's not a combo that says, "Look away."

But this was only the beginning. This was only Twat Waffle's arrival. So had I changed my tune that fast? Bono-y sunglasses + Entourage = I'll forsake him as an idol? No, no, no. *Pas du tout,* as the French say. Not at all. I wasn't turned off, just surprised. I stood at the ready with a water pitcher in my hand as Octavio, the back waiter, balanced a bottle of sparkling water in one hand and a bottle of still in the other. Twat Waffle settled into his seat a mere three feet from me and I worked to maintain my composure. "Sir?" I managed. My voice sounded like I'd just inhaled helium.

"Did you care for sparkling or still water?" Twat Waffle didn't answer me directly. Like something that should happen only in a movie—one of those moments to remind you that movies are not real life—Twat Waffle signaled a fedora wearer to lean in toward him, then whispered something in his ear. The fedora wearer answered, "We'll have sparkling water." Twat Waffle whispered something else. The fedora wearer added, "And a lemon wedge."

This was when my feet started hurting. You know how they say a mother could lift a car up off her child? How when your adrenaline gets going you're capable of these inhuman feats of strength and endurance? I'd been on my feet ten hours by the time I realized Twat Waffle was the type to use his entourage to communicate with the outside world, but before that, the excitement I'd harbored for meeting him facilitated a positive attitude and energy level that, after waiting tables for ten hours, was a feat as stupendous as, let's say, me bench pressing a Toyota. Once he toed the line of entourage-member-as-megaphone, however, everything changed. My excitement waned, my adrenaline dropped, and I became aware of my exhaustion. Speaking through one's entourage is like wearing a toe ring: so specific and psychotic a choice, it verifies the absence of a stable mind. Or rather, what *I* define to be a stable mind. When I see a person in a toe ring, I know all I need to know about her. I know she's spent time in either a sorority or a hippie enclave; I know she'll use the word *sweet* to mean "great." Similarly, a celebrity uses his entourage to communicate, and I know all I need to know about him: Regardless of his accomplishments, regardless of his public persona as a sensitive artist, regardless of the part he played in ushering a gal through her depressive tweenage slumps, he's headed to hell. And I do not mean the restaurant.

From there, things just got worse. I struggled to forgive Twat Waffle's antics, but every time I did, he'd undermine my efforts. I tried to write off the sparkling-water exchange as a fluke, but then it happened again when I asked if he cared for an alcoholic beverage. There were no "please"s and no "thank you"s. There were no solo trips to the bathroom; members of the entourage would clamor to accompany him there. I could feel my varicose veins bulging at my ankles. His sunglasses stayed on. I overheard him say, "Really, I am my own worst critic."

I thought, *I doubt it.*

To mitigate the physical pain of throbbing feet and the emotional pain of watching my idol fall from grace, I started calculating income. Twat Waffle plus six entourage members plus his fellow bandmates plus their respective entourages totaled a group of nineteen. Their bill, by three A.M., was an even two thousand dollars, and though they would not be charged a penny of this—Twat Waffle never received a bill when he dined at Hell—I figured this would warrant a two-hundred-dollar tip. Hopefully more like three. Four would be ideal—four would be 20 percent—but I realized that since they weren't being presented with a check and since they didn't seem mathematically inclined, figuring on two was best; I'd rather be pleasantly surprised than sadly disappointed. It's true I'd have to tip out half of that to Octavio and lose a bit to income tax, but still: A hundred bucks buys a lot of face waxes. So I thought about that for a while, and then Octavio and I played hangman on the back of a specials card, then a few rounds of "Who Would You Rather." (This is a game in which you select two people whom no one would ever want to sleep with and force the other participant to choose between them. For example: Who would you rather, your mom or your dad?) This made the time go faster.

By the time Twat Waffle and company got it together to leave, it was five A.M. I had been at Hell for thirteen hours. I'd been blatantly ignored and disregarded by everyone besides Octavio, who'd thought it was funny when I asked, "Who would you rather: me or Luigi?" I was considering certain sorts of homicide as a favor to society when *finally!* the group extinguished all their cigarettes (it's illegal to smoke in restaurants in New York, but

Luigi allows Twat Waffle and friends to disregard the rule) and marched toward the door to go home. I felt a flush of joy and thought, *At least it's over.* I turned back to the table to begin cleaning up but was stopped by the sight of Octavio, whose eyes had filled with tears.

"NO!" he screamed.

"No?" I asked. "No *what*?"

"NO DINERO!" he answered. It took fifteen seconds of a confusing back-and-forth for me to understand what Octavio was saying, for me to understand that Twat Waffle had not left us a tip.

Twat Waffle is a millionaire. A multi one. He owns a private jet. I know this because I saw it featured on *Iconoclasts*.

Twat Waffle had not been charged a penny for two thousand dollars' worth of food.

Twat Waffle had kept our staff of seven (waiter, back waiter, manager, food runner, three line cooks) on their feet for five extra hours. Just for him. A staff who logs, on average, a six-day workweek. Just for him. A staff who stayed around until five A.M. Just for him. Just so he could have his Madison Square Garden after party.

And he did so without tipping.

I must have looked to be on the verge of cardiac arrest, because when Darren emerged from the kitchen moments later he said, "Didn't tip?" I nodded. "Yeah." He sighed and said, "He never does. Well, at least you weren't here on the night he wanted waffles. C'mon, babe. Let's go home."

IT'S BEEN THREE YEARS since that first Twat Waffle encounter. I still work at Hell, and though I've been forced to wait on him several times since—I never volunteered again but the luck of the draw doesn't always save you—these encounters are never as traumatic as that first one. It's not that he's started remembering to tip or that his behavior has, in a more general sense, improved, it's just that now I know what I'm getting into. Now there's not the problem of fallen expectations. These evenings are always long and exhausting, and in addition to the games of hangman and "Who Would You Rather?" that I play to make the time go faster, I also use this time to think. I plot revenge scenarios. I mentally transport myself from Hell at two A.M. to Oprah Winfrey's big, beige couch. I imagine my feet propped up on an ottoman. I imagine she's brought me on to dish on bad celebrity behavior.

"Sara Barron's here!" she bellows like she bellows. "Tell us who's the worst!" The audience goes wild. They're jonesing for my gossip.

"Really?" I taunt. "You all really want to know?" It's worth noting that, in the context of this fantasy, my stomach's impossibly flat and I'm wearing a devastating pencil skirt and halter top and suddenly my breasts are perfect, plush C-cups. "Well, all right then," I say. "The worst of the worst is . . ."—and one of Twat Waffle's iconic '90s songs comes blaring through the studio speakers—". . . TWAT WAFFLE!"

The audience gasps! They cannot believe it!

"Oh yes," I confirm. "Oh *yes*."

"Twat Waffle?" Oprah asks. Oprah cannot believe it.

"Twat Waffle," I affirm, and I shake my head like it's as hard for me to say as it is for them to hear. "He doesn't tip or talk to people outside of his entourage. He forces line cooks into sixteen-hour workdays."

My appearance on *The Oprah Winfrey Show* is her highest rated of the season. My gospel spreads. Twat Waffle's record sales drop. A year goes by, and then they disappear completely—the world unites in opposition!—and since he can't rein in the heavy spending to which he's become accustomed, he goes bankrupt. Luigi drops him as a friend since he's not famous anymore. He's forced to get another job. He's forced to get *my* job at Hell, as a matter of fact, since I—of the impossibly flat stomach and C-cup breasts—don't work there anymore. I'm busy touring the country in my pencil skirt as I lecture on proper restaurant etiquette.

ACT V

antichrist

the days inn in madrid

In college, Maggie lived with a girl named Whitney, another aspiring actor. Whitney was very beautiful and used to receiving quite a lot of male attention, so when she arrived at acting school and found herself faced with a preponderance of Male Gay, she didn't know which way was up; the kick-ball breasts, the bee-stung lips, the raven hair swayed *no one*. Not anymore. Starved for attention, she decided that what she ought to do was give gay a try herself. So late one night Whitney got drunk, knelt at Maggie's bedside, and asked to have her breasts sucked. Maggie said no. Of course, the seed of awkwardness was sown then and there, and it more than likely would've grown like a tumor, so *thank god* it had been late enough, and both of them drunk enough, to pretend the whole thing hadn't happened. Left without perpetual male advances and surrounded by women disinterested in indulging her faux lesbian fantasies, Whitney was forced to forge platonic relationships instead. She and I forged a platonic relationship. We got along well seeing as how I was always in their dorm room, and also because we both liked shopping at Walgreens.

"Where were you this afternoon?" Maggie would ask. "I called three times and you never picked up."

"Whitney and I went to Walgreens to buy pantyhose," I'd answer. Or perhaps, "Whitney and I went to Walgreens to buy pumice stones."

"Did she flirt with you?"

"Not that I remember."

"There was no 'Let's make out'? No 'Suck my boobs'?"

"No 'Let's make out.' No 'Suck my boobs.' I think our gal is growing up."

Whitney and I have stayed friends over the years, and today she's one of the only people I know who's maintained a successful acting career. I'll give it to her that she, to quote Eugene Levy from *Waiting for Guffman,* "does INDEED have talent!"—she did a bang-up job on this Christopher Durang monologue back in 1999—but as far as I'm concerned her career success is thanks largely to her flawless physique. Her face helps, too. With big eyes and full lips, it's the sort to launch a thousand products: light-bulbs, plungers, diuretics. You name it, Whitney's booked a com-mercial to sell it. She scored an *Entourage* episode, a walk-on role on *Two and a Half Men,* and a Hallmark Channel made-for-TV movie. Most recently she wrapped a supporting role in *Pledge This!,* a full-length feature film. You probably haven't heard of *Pledge This!* and that's because it went straight to DVD. There's not a lot to say about it really, besides the fact that it stars this famous heiress/porn star—I'll call her Madrid Days Inn, because her name is not Madrid Days Inn—and that the script sounded like an uncreative child wrote it. The plot centers around two rival sororities on a Florida college campus and Madrid Days Inn plays the sorority president, a young woman who favors lingerie as clothing and says things like, "That girl better watch her back." Whitney plays a sorority sister from the rival sorority, and she and

Madrid get in a verbal sparring match at the start of the film. After that, high jinks ensue involving sex, a toilet, a makeover, and a pocket protector. The film runs one hour and twenty-one minutes, and at the end of it you're tempted to put a gun to your crotch and pull the trigger, just so you have something else to think about, just so you can be distracted from what you've voluntarily endured.

I Netflixed Whitney's film debut, and two days later she and I met up for coffee. We hadn't seen each other in ages and had a lot to catch up on. I announced a crush on a recent addition to the dishwashing department at Hell, and Whitney announced she'd decided to move to Los Angeles.

"I want to ride the wave of my *Pledge This!* success," she explained. "Madrid said that if I were in L.A., she could get me a spot on the next season of her reality show. How awesome is that?"

"Not," I answered. I thought it was not awesome because I thought Madrid Days Inn was not awesome. She has, over the years, inspired within me a deep and layered hatred, the sort a person ought to reserve for a murderer or sodomist—or, at the very least, a person she actually knows—but honestly, I've never been able to help myself. Her face gave me a headache. I hated her tan, I hated her hair. I hated her book. (This I once paged through masochistically in a Barnes & Noble, and—honest to god—it instructs young women, "Act ditzy! People will think you're adorable!" and then later, "Always act like you're on camera!") I hated her metabolism and I hated that despite my superior dancing skills, she was the one who got to shoot music videos alongside shapely naked men. I *hated* Madrid Days Inn, and I wasn't a big fan of Los Angeles either. It's true I'd only been there once, and while I did appreciate the cattycorner Jamba Juices alongside the experience of seeing my ex-boyfriend working at the Gap, my overall feeling was: *Dangerous people, dangerous place.* It didn't strike me as a good spot to move to, especially if the only item on one's itinerary was to ride an heiress/porn star's coattails.

I told Whitney, "Don't go to L.A. Please don't go." And then, because it seemed less complicated than addressing the real reasons I disapproved of the decision, I started singing a stanza from the 1992 smash single of the same name. "BABE, I LOVE YOU SOOOOO," I began, "AND I, I WANT YOU TO KNOW: THAT I-YYYYYY, I'M GONNA MISS YOUR LOOOOOOOVE! THE MINUTE YOU WALK OUT THAT DOOR!"

"Don't do that," said Whitney. "Do not sing."

"Fine," I agreed. "My point is, it's awful out there. Everyone's so shiny. Everyone wears expensive sweatpants!"

Whitney told me she would not make a decision based on someone else's sweatpants, and three weeks later she moved to L.A. This reduced our relationship to bimonthly e-mails in which I'd note the progress of my antidepressants and dishwasher flirtations and she, now fully enmeshed in Madrid Days Inn's entourage, would share stories of celebrity hobnobbing:

ME: *Just writing to say hi. I just went off my Lexapro—I decided that's what was making me so queasy. Besides that, not too much to report. I went out for beers last night with that dishwasher guy. He's cute but he always smells like cauliflower. For a while I thought maybe I was making it up, but then the other day at work my friend Lulu was like, "That dude smells like cauliflower!" And I was like, okay. Confirmed. It's not me. It's him. Anyway, how're things with you? —sb*

WHITNEY: *Hiiiiii!!! I'm SO sorry to hear you'd been feeling queasy: I know how much you hate that. Things here are CRAZY! I was out with Madrid last night and she got pissed at her Chihuahua, Tinkerfuck, after Tinkerfuck peed all over the front seat of her car. So she chucked her into the back seat where I was sitting and HIT ME IN THE FACE WITH HER!!! I woke up this morning covered in scratches!*

These e-mails went back and forth for months, me updating her when I switched to new fabric softener, exchanged numbers with a Hasidic real-estate agent, had the confrontation with the dishwasher about the cauliflower smell after gagging one night during an amorous encounter. Whitney, for her part, consistently offered up Madrid anecdotes. Whitney had moved to L.A. in November, and by January I'd learned the following:

1. Madrid Days Inn suffers from early-onset, female pattern baldness.

2. Madrid Days Inn sports nipples the size of silver dollars.

3. Madrid Days Inn calls waiters "Bitch."

4. Madrid Days Inn, after eating an In-N-Out burger she's chased with a half a flask of whiskey, has breath—and it's something to do with *her* specific body chemistry, I guess—that smells strikingly of post-asparagus pee.

Maybe it was wishful thinking, but I felt the tone of Whitney's e-mails suggested an awareness of Madrid's grotesqueness. I felt she understood that it's grotesque to chuck your purse dog like a dodgeball, that it's grotesque for breath to smell like pee, that it's grotesque to scream for your security guard when another person dances alongside you at a nightclub and steals the attention to which you think yourself solely entitled. The strange thing was that said awareness did not negate her interest—Madrid and Whitney spent countless nights a week together—and I had to wonder why. I mean, I understood the lure of celebrity was attractive, but this was no A-list situation we were dealing with; this was no Stamos. This was Madrid Days Inn, a universal laughingstock and cultural joke, the twenty-first-century Antichrist come to life as a gum-popping, Manolo-sporting, squash-colored leatherface. I imagined that being seen or photographed with her would be a source of embarrassment rather than pride, but Whitney disagreed. Or maybe not. Maybe Whitney was just having herself a grand old time, enjoying the free booze and easy club access, accruing funny stories for her friends back in New York, in a town where she knew no one. Yes. That was it. Of course it was.

Then one day I came home from work, took off my North Face boots, put on my glasses, and sat down to check my e-mail. There was a bunch of spam, an update on a Keyspan payment, a message from my mother informing me of her colonoscopy preparations, and a message from Whitney. This last one read, "You will not believe it, but when I was out last night I accidentally woke up Tinkerfuck when Tinkerfuck was sleeping and—I SWEAR TO GOD!—Madrid tried to slap me! I blocked her but she tried!"

I couldn't take it anymore. As someone raised to believe you *never* hit another person unless that person gives you AIDS, physical violence is my final straw. I feared Whitney was losing perspective, and this fear warranted the question: "WHY ARE YOU STILL SPENDING TIME WITH HER?!" (And I used all caps just as I've done here so she'd understand the severity of my concern.)

The next day Whitney wrote back: "Calm down. I only e-mail you the crazy stuff, but really, she's super cool! I promise. You just have to get to know her."

I took a shower after that sentence appeared in my inbox. I used the Brillo-y side of my kitchen sponge to exfoliate until my skin was raw, until I felt a bit less filthy by association. Whitney had gone mental, clearly. "YOU'VE LOST YOUR MIND!" I wrote.

"Very funny," she responded. "No I haven't. The next time Madrid's in New York we'll all hang out and you'll see what I mean. She's super sweet. I miss you!"

I was appalled by this suggestion. How could she think I'd disgrace myself that way?! Or encourage her self-destructive behavior?! I had a spine, after all, and though I didn't like to use it, this seemed a good occasion. I would not encourage the cult of celebrity surrounding Madrid Days Inn! I would not indulge her with my company! I would be the one who took a stand!

But then I got the e-mail with the official invite.

"Madrid's coming to New York next week," Whitney wrote me

one month later, "and I'm coming with her, and I *so* want us to chill! Let's plan on Sunday night."

I must be honest and admit I wanted desperately to go. This impulse shocked me—I would've guessed it would've made me need another shower—and I tried to ignore it. I typed the words *How could you think* and deleted them. My want to be included was too strong, and perhaps I should've let this fact afford me some insight into Whitney's actions and desires, but I preferred to differentiate between us: *I* wanted a night out with Madrid Days Inn not because I'd like her, I decided, but because I wanted proof. The next time Whitney dropped the bomb of "super cool" or "super sweet" I wanted hard evidence from which to pull so I could say, "No. She's not. She FUPA-punched me that one night when I outdanced her." Firsthand experience would strengthen my argument. I typed a cold, "Fine. Just tell me when and where."

There's a spot in Soho called Downtown Cipriani where celebrities go on Sunday nights to perform karaoke. That's where I was told to meet Madrid and Whitney, and I did so outfitted in this backless Nicole Miller number I'd bought on sale at Bloomingdales earlier that month. (Marked down from $295 to $70! *That* was a good day.) Guarding the entrance was a hulk of a man in a gorgeous suit he spoiled with a ponytail that hung between his shoulders. Correction: It *would* have hung between his shoulders, but because he swept it *over* his shoulders, really, it hung against his sternum. I'd been instructed via text message to tell him, "Hey. Are you Joaquin? Wassup, Joaquin. I'm Sara. I'm meeting Madrid upstairs, cool?" Then Joaquin would answer, "Cool," and I'd proceed through a dining room, up a flight of stairs, down a short corridor, and into a room. Partitioned off in the back of this room there'd be a banquette, and in that banquette there'd be Whitney and Madrid. All this had been clearly mapped out for me, but what I hadn't expected was to see Whitney *atop* Madrid. Not recycling her old lesbian moves necessarily; it was more an intense sort of fawning. Whitney was draped across one side of Madrid's body (like if you spooned someone

217

while sitting upright) and whispering in her ear. She screamed when she saw me—"OH MY GOD! HI!"—but did not get up lest she lose her spot atop her tanned and balding throne.

I inched toward them through the crowd and noticed all eyes were on me by virtue of the fact that all eyes were on Madrid; she served as the room's focal point, a fact that surprised me. Based on Whitney's description, I'd expected Downtown Cipriani to be a celebrity *scene*. I expected Madrid to be just one recognizable face out of many; I expected I'd snag a glance at a Colin Farrell, a Nick Lachey, an Adrian Grenier. I pictured Adrian spotting me from across the room, noting my low cheekbones, pointing me out to his band of celebrity brothers—Elijah Wood? Kevin Connolly? Tara Reid?—and saying, "Wow. A *real* woman. How refreshing." Then, drawn as he was to my realness, he'd saunter toward me, and over the course of an hour we'd discuss topics as insightful as Hollywood's plastic surgery obsession. My Adrian fantasy boiled down to the acquisition of attention, but again, I distinguished between Whitney and myself with the rationale that my fantasy was based on *sexual* attention. I wanted Adrian Grenier to notice me because he had a penis; the HBO series was secondary.

Adrian Grenier was not at Downtown Cipriani the night that I attended, however. No one famous was save for Madrid, a couple of contestants I'd seen on *The Bachelor,* and Keith Richards's daughter, whose name escapes me. It was a tragic who's who resulting in Madrid Days Inn as the decisive center of attention. Whitney may have been the one who was on her, but a dozen others flanked every available angle, laughing when she laughed, pouting when she pouted.

I struggled through the crowd and sat down beside them so Whitney could introduce us.

"MADRID!" she screamed over the Right Said Fred karaoke favorite "I'm Too Sexy," "THIS IS SARA!"

"Hello," I said.

"Hello," she said. "Nice dress."

Exchanging pleasantries with Madrid Days Inn while the song "I'm Too Sexy" blasts in your ears feels blatantly apocalyptic. You think the world is ending. You feel fear, but then your survivalist instinct kicks in. Mine said, "Flee the scene." I pointed to my small intestine.

"My IBS!" I yelled. "It's flaring up!"

"WHAT?" screamed Whitney.

"MY IBS! IT'S FLARING UP! WHERE'S THE NEAREST BATHROOM?"

Whitney motioned back toward the entrance but Madrid made the move to stop her. "Where are you going?" she asked. And then before I could respond, she said, "I think you're fucking hot. I think your dress is fucking hot."

It was like that old Groucho Marx quip about never wanting to be a member of the club that will have you as a member: Madrid Days Inn must have sensed I was the only person there unwilling to focus their attention on her, and this was just the thing to make her want it. Well, lucky for Madrid, I'd already used my spine once that month; twice would have been excessive. "Really?" I asked. "You like it?"

The heiress/porn star delivered unto me a compliment and immediately, *instinctually,* I decided that maybe she wasn't so bad. Three years invested in raging and loathing, three years after having bestowed upon her the superlative *Most* Mortal Enemy, and all was lost in an instant. A fleck of her attention in an environment where it was all anyone wanted, and everything changed. When in the past I'd heard Madrid Days Inn on E! or VH1 using her token descriptor "hot," I'd pictured her in hell exploding groin-first into flames. But when she said it to *me,* when *I* was the object of approval, it sounded different. It sounded charming. The scrap of attention kicked my endorphins into gear and left me blind and happy.

Over the years, I've come to realize that happiness done right leaves a person without ample reason to complain. I simply cannot live like that, and so, on the occasions wherein I find myself feeling vaguely satisfied, I like to undermine the sentiment by examining the reasons why, e.g., "I feel happy. Because Madrid Days Inn paid attention to me. Why does attention from Madrid Days Inn make me feel happy?" (I see Sheila Epstein twice a week now. I assume this has something to do with my "instinctive" way of thinking.) Attention had come part and parcel with Madrid's compliment, and attention is the drug that always sets me on the road to Happy Town. I'm a whore for attention, one with holes made deep and wide by insecurity, holes hungry for filling by approval. It's not the most distinctive trait, but what bowled me over when I considered it in this particular context, was the source. I'd previously considered myself to be at least a little bit discriminating. But here I learned, in point of fact, I'm not. I would take it from wherever I could get it. And why? Why did I care? What is an heiress/porn star's approval really worth, after all? Rationally, I knew nothing, but the irrational kicks in at a place like Downtown Cipriani. You're stuck between four windowless walls and so the focal point becomes whatever A/B/C-list celebrity is on hand, whichever one's most famous. Here, Madrid was the center of attention and she paid *me* attention and since attention is my drug of choice, I got immediately hooked. I was ready and willing to do whatever I had to for more.

So I shouted, "Thanks! That means *so* much coming from you!"

And then Whitney piped in, "Sara's a *huge* fan, Madrid. Like, *huge!*"

And I nodded. "Huge! I saw you in *Pledge This!* You were, um, hello?! Awesome! *SO AWESOME!*"

For the most part, verbal exchanges are re-created in this sort of nonfiction context as best the author can remember them: The *essence* of a dialogue is given to help get to the point, clarify a character, etc. But in this particular instance, I'm rendering the conversation verbatim. I've neither nipped nor tucked a word. What I said *exactly* was: "I saw you in *Pledge This*! You were, um, hello?! Awesome! *SO AWESOME!*"

When you begin to feel your soul slipping slowly out from your behind onto the velvet VIP banquette at Downtown Cipriani, you decide that all is lost. There is no chance for redemption, you realize, and so why *not* go down in a blaze of shame? After I told Madrid that I thought her *Pledge This!* performance was "so awesome," I went on to say, "Your hair looks amazing! How did you get it to do that?" and "Oh my god! You are hilarious!" I think I might also have described some aspect of her as being "fierce." I spent the remainder of my evening like this, and whether it all lasted minutes or hours, I don't know, so high was I on what Madrid kept giving back: glances, giggles, emptily flirtatious strokes of my knee, shots of Malibu rum, a handful of gestures that woven together played a sad refrain in my mind, a dozen looks that struck at the sick, self-absorbed center of my Tootsie Pop: *You're special you're special you're special*. I wish it had been something less tired or cliché, but no: *My* internal beat struck the rhythm of those three pathetic syllables to make not a statement, but a plea.

Eventually, Madrid Days Inn stood up from her Sara/Whitney sandwich—a heavily tweezed man had requested her autograph and she graciously obliged—and freed as I was from our compulsive give-and-take, I had a moment to reflect. I could step outside myself to see:

I was the Antichrist.

I'd come to confirm judgments and suspicions and, in so doing, chase a sense of superiority. But then I'd tripped and fallen on the unanticipated force of heiress/porn star celebrity, and now I couldn't get up. Worse than Whitney was I. Worse than Madrid Days Inn herself! For at least they lacked my pretense. At least if Whitney kissed an ass until her lips went dry, she hadn't claimed for years that such actions were beneath her. Pit my hypocrisy in a cage match against Madrid Days Inn's entitlement, and I fear I could've won.

What do you do when forced into self-reflection by an heiress/porn star, when she succeeds in teaching you a lesson? Flee the scene? Change your ways? Schedule an appointment with your therapist Sheila Epstein? You do nothing so dramatic. You're incapable of such progressive actions, for you possess no moral gumption nor strength of metaphoric spine. You would have avoided your problems in the first place if you did. So you reach for the Malibu rum (Downtown Cipriani provides bottle service, hence your access to it) and you pour yourself a shot into a champagne flute filled with pineapple juice. You drink until Madrid's breathy giggles start sounding sweet instead of sickening, until you can convince yourself again of your own superiority. Until your judgment is too clouded to see that as a lie.

ACKNOWLEDGMENTS

Many thanks are due to the following people for their help in shaping, improving, and/or inspiring this book. Mostly, though, just for constant contradictions of its title:

Samuel Barron, Joseph Barron, Lynn Handelman Barron, and Natalie Handelman. Amanda Rowan, Amy Shearn, Andrew Ranaudo, Bethany Ruch, Carl Ferrero, Carrie Thornton, Celestina Villanueva, Elisabeth Weed, Erin Fritch, Gary Huddleston, Jeffrey Cutaiar, Joseph Zvejnieks, Jon Fisch, Kimberly Ahlheim, Kimberlee Auerbach, Lourdes Benavides, Maggie McBrien, Mat Sanders, Michelle Newman, Patricia Lemon, and Rachel Sher.

ABOUT THE AUTHOR

SARA BARRON's work has appeared on Showtime's *This American Life,* on National Public Radio's *Weekend Edition,* and at the HBO comedy festival. She lives in Brooklyn, New York.